Martina Unauthorized

Adrianne Blue argued for equal prize-money for women at Wimbledon before most players were willing to go out on a limb publicly. As an investigative reporter, she uncovered the hypocrisy that allowed millions of pounds' worth of Wimbledon tickets to be sold on a VIP-only black market just yards from centre court. A *Sunday Times* correspondent, she has written on sport and contemporary literature for the *Washington Post*, the *New Statesman*, the *Independent* and *Cosmopolitan*. Formerly special consultant to the women's tennis tour TV programmes, Britain's leading writer in the field of women's sport is an American who lives in London. Her most recent book, *Queen of the Track*, was named 'the athletics book of the decade'.

D1055149

Martina Unauthorized

ADRIANNE BLUE

VICTOR GOLLANCZ

LONDON

For my grandmother, Percha Thaler

First published in Great Britain 1994
by Gollancz/Witherby

First Gollancz Paperback published 1995
by Victor Gollancz
An imprint of the Cassell Group
Wellington House, 125 Strand, London WC2R 0BB

A catalogue record for this book is
available from the British Library

ISBN 0 85493 253 4

Typeset by
Rowland Phototypesetting Ltd,
Bury St Edmunds, Suffolk
Printed in Great Britain by
Cox & Wyman Ltd, Reading

Contents

Acknowledgements

My thanks to Martina Navratilova for what help she did give me, and for not standing in my way.

Many who were there as the events of her private or professional life unfolded have been generous with their recollections. I have often relied on their testimony. I want to thank in particular: Tracy Austin, Dianne Beal, Vaclav Bloha, Paul Blue, Radka Bobkova, Rita Mae Brown, Jim Courier, Margaret Court, Jaroslav Drobny, Ian Dusek, Chris Evert, Steffi Graf, Sandra Haynie, Gert Kievan, Jan Kodes, Billie Jean King, Petr Korda, Ana Leaird, Adam Mars-Jones, Conchita Martinez, Judy Nelson, Vera Novakova, Jana Novotna, Jan Pospichal, Arantxa Sanchez Vicario, Jiri Severa, Pam Shriver, Jiri Skoch, Josef Slajs, Pavel Slozil, Helena Sukova, Brian Tobin, Vlasta Vopickova, Vaclav Zitko and those who didn't want to be named.

L'Equipe Anglaise which includes two Americans and a South African: Lyn Allison, Merilyn Blue, Madeleine Harmsworth, Matthew Hoffman, Jane Kirwan and Mike Thompson.

Of my other colleagues and friends: Tracey Dawn Bates, Geraldine Baum, Rex Bellamy, Karen Black, Diane Cleaver, Bud Collins, Phil Daniels, Tina Davila, Dudley Doust, Judith Elian, Alexandra Erskine and her staff, Teresa Garfield, Giles Gordon, Ginger Hjelmaa, Candice Hogan, David Irvine, Liz Knights, Robert Kirby, Sue Henny, Marie Kovarnova, Rose Lambert,

John Lovesey, Sara Maitland, Anne McArthur, Annie Mejean, Joan Minogue, Sue Mott, Nick Pitt, Mari Roberts, Peter Roberts, Mimi Sanderson, June Shanahan, Michele Slung, Hana Vockova, Katrina Whone, Richard Wigmore.

Using the methods of modern biography I have dramatized events during matches and elsewhere, never going beyond the statements made by the principals in interviews with me or with one of my colleagues, or the personal recollections of people present at the time the event occurred.

Thanks also to the Czech Tennis Federation, the Daily Telegraph Reference Library and the News International Reference Library, to *The Advocate, Architectural Digest*, Associated Newspapers, the *Daily Telegraph, Gay Times*, the *New York Times, Sports Illustrated, The Times*, the *Sunday Times, USA Today*, the *Washington Post* and BBC Television.

Prologue

A Corridor of Truth

Twenty minutes before the interview, for which I had been waiting all week, my tape recorder broke. I had dropped the machine the day before, but it seemed none the worse. It had worked last night. Listening to Martina's voice, which I had taped at the press conference, I puzzled over what it was about the Czech language that made its natives speak English with something at once a monotone and a singsong. In Prague in April, I had heard the same odd intonation. This was to be a short interview, but one I regarded as crucial and wanted on tape. I tried new batteries, then a fresh cassette. The tape recorder was dead. 'This is a nightmare,' I muttered. It was too late to buy another.

I was in Paris at the French Open where I knew things were not going well for Martina either. Five days earlier she had been defeated in the first round and uncharacteristically smashed her racket. After a lifetime of famous victories had come what would surely be remembered as a famous defeat. It was May, 1994. With her last Wimbledon coming up in less than a month in June, Martina knew she was playing pretty badly. Covering the court she was slower by two paces than in her prime.

Wondering if there was any hope for my tape recorder, I surveyed the big, deserted press room. There were eighteen television monitors no one was watching, and just four people. One, writing in Korean on his Apple Powerbook, stopped to have a go at my tape recorder, but couldn't revive it. The three French journalists didn't look up. In poor French, I threw myself on their mercy. Dennis, from French radio, whom I had never seen before and never saw again, lent me a complicated broadcast-quality recorder, and quickly showed me how to use it. 'You must be sure to get her to do a test first, and listen with the earphones,' he said. 'I hope the batteries work.'

I reached the operatives of the Women's Tennis Association (WTA) just in time and they rushed me into the players' lounge and up the stairs. 'Hide your press badge, we're going to try to get you through.' The three organizations running the show at the French Open were, like Machiavellian medieval principalities, continually jostling each other for hegemony. This particular forbidden corridor of the player sanctuary led to the courts where Martina, who had stayed on to play the doubles, had a practice scheduled in a very few minutes. It was not, I realized as I was ushered into the presence, an auspicious moment. But there she was, Martina Navratilova, the woman I had been waiting for and watching. Dressed for tennis, she had her racket in hand.

Even before I spoke, her coach Craig Kardon, in his perennial peaked cap, looked at his watch and thumped it with a forefinger, motioning her to hurry. And Martina, like a race horse at the starting gate, seemed to be champing at the bit, eyes blinkered, nostrils figuratively flaring.

Eight years ago in Eastbourne I had noticed that same look of distant concentration. Those eyes that didn't blink. Was it because they were focused on destiny, or because they were staring down defeat? On this her farewell tour, things had been going badly. Tears instead of the traditional triumph in Chicago, and now for the first time since 1976, she had been knocked out in the first round of a grand slam.

Watching her practise for that disastrous first-round match, I had noticed that she had what appeared to be a slight varicosity on the back of one leg. Now, as we stood face to face, I noticed another tiny imperfection, something akin to a mole, on her cheek. One of the pleasures of sports writing is the physical beauty of the athletes you meet, most of whom exude grace and vigour and youth. For a moment I thought Martina looked remarkably unhealthy. Then I corrected myself. She did not look unhealthy, but when compared to the five-foot eleven-inch willowy nineteen-year-old Mary Pierce, or to the big, buxom Conchita Martinez, twenty-two, Martina looked old. Pam Shriver, at thirty-one the other grand dame of the circuit, referred to herself as haggard. Martina was pushing thirty-eight. This meant everything she did was harder. And it might hurt more.

She deserved, like a character in a William Faulkner novel, a lot of credit just for enduring. And she had done so much more than that. The most famous sportswoman in the world was the greatest female tennis player the world had ever known.

A few days earlier, Martina had kept the man from *Sports Illustrated* waiting a long time after her doubles match. 'What's taking so long?' he asked.

'Old body,' joked Ana Leaird, the WTA publicity director. Then she added, 'I didn't say that.' Ana Leaird went to school with Chris Evert and was a bridesmaid at her wedding. She knows Martina from way back. Martina was a good friend of Chris in the first stages of their great sixteen-year rivalry. 'We're still friends,' Martina assured me later. Ana Leaird knows Martina long and well. She was indeed delayed by her body and by the fact that during the post-match massage she was also undergoing an interview at the hands of Judith Elian of the sports newspaper *L'Equipe*. Elian had been in the business about twenty-one years, as long as Martina, who wasn't talking privately to anyone she didn't already really know.

The WTA was helping me, although not much, because of the profile I was writing for the *Sunday Times*. Had I told them I was also writing a book they might not have let me anywhere near Martina. People writing books about tennis can feel the

12

ranks close. I also had some information I thought would be of use to Martina.

Martina Navratilova is a compact, medium-sized, medium-breasted woman whom British photographers use their lenses to portray as massive. She looked to me, though, as if she had put on weight. Gert, the pre-eminent Martina fan, now elevated to the rank of practice session ball girl, would insist this was merely an illusion. 'The strict vegetarian diet has made her lighter.' Gert had a VIP pass which identified her as one of the 'Famille Navratilova'. It was Martina who had arranged it.

Martina Navratilova has charm when she wants to and possesses perhaps the finest sense of humour in tennis, but she did not want this interview. It had been urged on her by the officials of the WTA.

'You have your pre-Wimbledon dreams,' I began, 'well I have just had my Navratilova nightmare—'

'I have lots of dreams, but not for public knowledge,' she replied. Her words seemed to slap my wrist. It wasn't always thus. The Martina of old liked to relate her dreams. *The Times* habitually reported her pre-Wimbledon dream, and *Newsweek* once ran three. In one of them, poisonous snakes are wrapped around the key to a Ferrari, but Martina gets the key anyway, and drives off. I hadn't been asking for a dream. But I should have known better. One doesn't make idle conversation with legends in a hurry.

'Say something into the microphone, please,' I said hastily, donning the earphones. 'I was told I had to test this first.'

'One two three.'

'Again.'

'One two three.'

It seemed to be working. 'How much time have I got?'

'Well you wanted five minutes, that's how much time you've got. I'm practising at two-thirty.'

'I wanted much more time.' I had a list of twenty-two questions in my pocket, and quite a few more in my head.

'That's not what I was told.' Again her tone lashed.

She knew of my mission to write a major profile. That was why I had been given the time. But five minutes seemed an insult and a nonsense. It would be hard, I thought, to accomplish anything at all.

And so we began what would be a short, sharp little conversation, she visibly restive, I becoming more so.

There was no time to build rapport, so I got right to it. 'Do you know that if you wanted to have dual citizenship you probably could? The Americans have changed the law.' Previously the United States did not allow its nationals to hold a second passport. 'I'm an American and I live in Britain. I'm applying and some of my friends have already got it.'

She didn't seem terribly interested.

I continued, 'Drobny has his Czech citizenship back.'

'Hmm.'

The first famous Czech tennis defector Jaroslav Drobny, the Wimbledon champion of 1954, had shown me his green Czech passport in Prague. 'In Britain I'm British,' he said. 'Here I'm Czech.' Drobny, who defected in 1949, travelled on Egyptian papers until he was finally allowed to become British ten years later. He lives in London. His two visits home had both been since the Communist Party was thrown out in the 1989 Velvet Revolution. Martina had met Drobny, also a left-hander, on one of her first trips to Wimbledon. She too had been back to Prague recently, but no one had given her a Czech passport.

'Would you be interested?' I asked.

'I haven't thought about it since I didn't know about it.' Then she said firmly, 'There is no reason for me to have it.'

But I felt she was interested in the fact that the Czechs had decided officially to let bygones be bygones with Drobny. It meant they might with her.

Later, she did look into it. Drobny had wanted a Czech passport only for sentimental reasons. That would be Martina's reason, too. But it was too late. If only Martina's advisers had investigated the possibilities earlier she almost certainly could easily have had both passports. Now ex-Czechs who wanted their citizenship back would have to give up their other citizenship. Martina, of course, would never do that. One day a new law might be passed. Meanwhile, she had missed out. Partly to compensate, perhaps, six months after our conversation Martina was proclaimed an honorary citizen of her childhood home, the village of Revnice.

In some ways Martina is as American as violence and apple pie. From the first time she saw the United States, she says, she felt American. In the first house she owned in Texas, she used to spend a lot of time watching soap operas to improve her English. Martina is also deeply Czech. In an America that has closed its doors, she will always be regarded as an immigrant. To the Czechs who have so recently opened theirs, she will always be Czech.

'I understand you wanted to talk to me about something with the Czech Federation,' Martina said.

'Right. I understand you offered them money when you were there for the Federation Cup in 1986 and the Communists wouldn't let them take it.'

'No, it's not true. Why would I offer them money when they don't even recognize me as a human being?'

'Well, what surprised me, and I wondered if it surprised you, they were terribly pleased to see you and they all recognize you as Czech.'

'Yeah, of course they did.'

'I thought they'd be angry at you but they weren't.'

'The Czechs aren't angry. The Communists were angry.'

'Even when you left? Did your parents have trouble?'

'No, I was a hero to them because I stuck it to the system.'

'That's what everybody said and I was amazed because I lived in a country where people thought they were part of the system.'

'Yeah but you wouldn't want to be part of the system in Czechoslovakia. The system kept you from doing anything.'

To the Czechs, she continues to be a hero – the common American usage – or heroine, the more old-fashioned word I prefer. To many in the West she is a heroine too, and some of

15

those who do not applaud her principles respect her courage in defending them. But not all, especially in the United States. Born-again America is not a place where one calmly agrees to differ. She has been denounced from the pulpit by fundamentalists and has had some of the most horrendous press ever, and not just in America. So it is not surprising that sometimes she appears to be distant and defensive, looking over her shoulder, as she was now, at Craig, who has been there just out of earshot all this time and was again looking at his wrist and motioning with his forefinger.

'Listen, Martina, I want to tell you something. I'm a specialist in women's sport. I've written a number of books about women's sport, and I've been thinking about it for ten years, and I've decided I'm going to write a book about your career. I just want you to know. I don't expect you to have the time to give me very much help but I want you to know.'

'So you're just another person writing a book about me.'

'Yes, just another person. If I get in touch with your assistant, can I ask her some questions and you get them back to me, is that possible?'

'I don't think I'll be happy to help you write your book, because first of all I'm doing books on my own, so I'd rather be concentrating on that than helping somebody else put a book together on me.'

'All right, I understand that.' The books on her own were three tennis mysteries being written for her by a professional writer. As Martina herself revealed later in a television interview with Cliff Richard, 'I didn't get the idea and I didn't write it. The idea came from the writer.'

'But anyway,' I continued, 'I want you to know that I'm on your side and thank you for the five minutes.'

'I understand that. Thanks very much.' She was backing away towards Craig and out of the door.

'Martina hears book, England.' Ana Leaird shakes her head. 'The British press doesn't exactly have a very good reputation.'

'I'm not from the tabloid press.'

'I know,' Ana says, 'or you wouldn't have gotten in to see her at all. I've been in my job for fifteen years. I checked on you.' A large part of Ana's job is keeping players away from the press while giving the optical illusion of proximity. Tennis is the only major sport in which American journalists are barred from the locker room. Journeys into the players' lounges are carefully regulated too. At Wimbledon, although sports writers may enter at pre-arranged moments, the lounge is entirely off-limits to news reporters who might see or say too much. To the public at large this protection of the players seems like no bad thing, but if you want full facts without the PR, you have to have access.

The world of tennis is run like Fort Knox. Players have to come to press conferences but they do not have to do face-to-face interviews. The argument can be made that there is enough access at press conferences, where Martina certainly is willing to discuss just about anything from the O. J. Simpson murder case, to when she first realized she was a lesbian, to what time she gets up in the morning. One needed a private interview only to guard scoops or to deliver a personal message like mine about this book.

The first time I had come within talking distance of Martina Navratilova, that time at Eastbourne in 1986, I asked her how tennis had changed the image of women. The words I quoted in a *Vogue* article were, 'Tennis has opened the door to many athletes and would-be athletes, and changed the image of women in sport.' She was already speaking in soundbites, as any good interviewee should. Tennis had led the way in the physical revolution that a whole generation of women who jogged, played tennis or went to aerobics classes had experienced. But then tennis went cautious.

As my ninety-year-old uncle who used to be communist would say, 'Russia led the way, and Russia lost the way.' So, apparently, has tennis, which at times seems overly concerned with its image. After that conversation with Ana, in which she assured me she had told her staff to continue to cooperate, the WTA seemed to me politely unhelpful, especially when they learned I had talked with Billie Jean King about hers and Martina's sexuality.

After the interview in Paris whenever I saw her Martina was never very cordial, but she was cordial. Perhaps she realized that I didn't have to tell her I was writing a book. Since I was also reporting for the *Sunday Times* at Wimbledon, I could well have kept the book undercover. As I would explain to Ana Leaird when the WTA seemed to be stonewalling me, 'I didn't have to tell her, Ana. I knew it wasn't smart.'

I was not unhappy that the biography would be unauthorized. Although it meant that I had to check very carefully whatever the people who had been important in her professional and personal life revealed to me, it also gave me a valuable freedom. Because what I wrote would not be subject to Martina's approval, I would be free to write the truth as I saw it. The only way to get an uncensored account of the life of a living person is in an unauthorized biography. I would not be part of the publicity machine.

On the whole book authors can afford to be more forthright than tennis correspondents. To maintain their regular access, tennis correspondents have to keep things fairly sweet. Like all sports writers, they know better than to ask too many pointed questions and to ask them carefully. There were even a fair number who published the wholesome non-story the WTA was pushing about the first American teenager since Jennifer Capriati to enter the top ten in the world rankings. Lindsay Davenport stayed home in California to go to her high-school prom instead of playing Eastbourne which would have given her pre-Wimbledon practice on grass. This story was the WTA's answer to the Capriati drug-taking scandal and to the recent criticism of tennis dropouts. Young Jennifer went to school largely by fax. At top level, though, tennis has always been a matter of careful priorities. Chris Evert skipped her high-school graduation ceremony to play tennis in England. Martina Navratilova dropped out.

At the press conferences, and there were a great many, whenever I asked my questions along with the rest of the hyenas, Martina answered thoughtfully and more thoroughly than one might have expected. As she herself would say at that last Wimbledon, 'I have been telling the truth for twenty years.' She felt she had nothing to hide.

Anyway, how could she hide anything? On the day after her defection, she invited the media in for a press conference. Amid the notoriety of an unusual 'divorce' from Judy Nelson, she agreed to be interviewed head to head on American network television by Barbara Walters, who was known for probing questions. Almost like family in the stands watching intently, the press and television have borne witness to Martina's greatest traumas and triumphs – to her life, her loves, her penchant for acting on what she sees to be the truth.

It is important that we know the whole truth about Winston Churchill or, say, Princess Diana, both subjects of recent revelatory biography, because that knowledge informs our sense of history and our sense of reality. No thrones have threatened to topple in the case of Martina, but hers is a life in which the personal has often indeed been political. It is also a life that has been immensely public. Public people make a bargain with the media. They obtain fame and its perquisites (power, money and immortality) and pay with a loss of privacy.

With that true albeit self-serving disclaimer, let us now listen in on two private conversations which changed a 'marriage', a friendship and tennis history.

Martina seemed so vulnerable that day. 'There were times where she was so confident, she could do anything,' recalls Judy Nelson, 'and then there were times where she was so vulnerable and she was so afraid, so frightened.' On Amelia Island, in Florida, that April day in 1989, Judy could sense that fear lurking. In the past year Martina had failed to win a single grand slam tournament. In her sad eyes, more brown than hazel, Judy searched for a glimmer of hope. She couldn't find it. Martina was wondering if it was time to quit.

'OK,' said Judy, 'you're scared, you're tired, you're burned out. What do you want to do?'

Martina wanted to make tennis history. But, she mused, 'How can somebody coach me to win a ninth Wimbledon when I'm the only one that's ever won that many?'

'Think of somebody in the whole world.'

Martina couldn't.

'You have a wonderful coach in Craig Kardon,' Judy said. 'He's a gentle, kind human being, he's like a brother to you. You're getting there but you're not able to make it happen. Why?'

'Well, Craig's never even played a final at Wimbledon. How can he know what I'm feeling when I get there but can't make it happen?'

'OK, think about what you're saying, Martina. You're saying he hasn't been there. He hasn't felt what you feel. So who *has* felt what you feel? Who has been there? Who has tried, and who has succeeded?'

Martina said, 'Well, Billie Jean.'

— 1 —

The Line of Succession

'Help.' The flat voice on the telephone sounds faintly European.

'Who is this?' Billie Jean King asks. 'Is it Martina? It sounds like your voice.'

'Yes.' Billie Jean can hear the tears. 'I don't know what to do.'

Billie Jean King has always been envious of Martina's tears. 'She always cries when she loses. She cries easier than anybody.' Billie Jean King has a hard time crying. Billie — her friends and her assistants often call her Billie — feels it all in her stomach. 'Well, Martina does feel it in her stomach, but she is able to cry quickly, which is great, always letting off that pressure and that steam, which is good.'

Martina is calling from Amelia Island in Florida where, as Billie already knows because she was watching the tennis on TV when the phone rang, she has just been pulverized in the semi by Gabriela Sabatini. But that defeat is just symptomatic of the problem. Martina is playing terrible tennis. It is April, 1989. Less than three months before Wimbledon. If Martina doesn't pull herself together soon, it will be too late to capture another Wimbledon singles championship, the one that will etch her name indelibly in tennis history. No one has ever won Wimbledon nine times. Martina and Helen Wills Moody, who won her last Wimbledon half a century ago in an easier era,

21

are tied with eight. Now Martina tells Billie she wants one last chance at becoming the greatest in the history of the game.

'Could you help me? I will fire all of my coaches, [fire] Craig, I will do everything . . .'

'No, no, no, you can't fire anybody,' retorts Billie. 'Else I won't help you. That's the first thing. But what do you want?'

'I just need help.' Martina knows her tennis is drowning. She hopes her old friend Billie, who is the smartest and most energetic woman in tennis, will throw her a lifeline.

Billie can understand Martina's desperation. It was what she herself had felt when it began to look like it was too late for her to claim a less important record. Only six of Billie's Wimbledon titles were at singles, but she had won a total of thirteen women's and mixed doubles. To claim the combined overall record of twenty, she had needed just one more. With a 22-year-old Martina as her doubles partner, in 1979, at the age of thirty-five, Billie won a last Wimbledon doubles title. Billie wishes she had won a couple more to protect the record. She believes it would have been possible if Martina hadn't dumped her as a doubles partner.

The thought still makes Billie Jean King's voice tighten. 'I was upset with Martina at the time. Martina dropped me as her doubles partner when we'd made a promise that we would be doubles partners throughout my career, as long as I was playing well enough.' And she believes she was playing well enough.

But that once agonizing disappointment is water under the bridge in what has been a long and intimate friendship. Anyway, Billie blames Rita Mae for Martina's decision to end the partnership. Billie believes that Rita Mae Brown, Martina's lover at the time, urged her to stop playing doubles with Billie to improve Martina's chance of surpassing Billie's record. Billie knows how important records are to Martina. Rita Mae would later tell me she played no part in Martina's decision. Billie remains unconvinced.

'Could you help me?' Billie hears Martina saying. 'I don't know what to do.'

Billie takes a breath, and answers quickly, 'OK.'

Temporarily Martina Navratilova has been saved from drowning. That telephone call was an important unreported moment in tennis history, for in it one great Wimbledon champion agreed to help another potentially greater champion eclipse her in the hearts and memories of the fans, in the purple prose of sports writers and in the record books. Her SOS had been answered, but whether or not Martina could be tugged to victory was still a great unknown. In the wake of the powerful Steffi Graf, it would be easy to capsize the dream. I think they both knew the odds were poor. Psychologically, the voyage might be perilous. Martina's 32-year-old body might give out. Only one thing was fairly certain. Martina's game would get worse before it got better. If it got better.

If Craig Kardon feels threatened by the arrival of Billie, he doesn't show it at the first joint coaching session in May. The dark hair crammed into the peaked cap, those long eyelashes, Craig, who has a face that reminds you of Tony Curtis in the old movies, knows his player's feelings are more important than his own. If this is what Martina wants, Craig will go along with it, just as he hits with her when she needs him to, and keeps her on schedule, and mixes her special drink for her when she wants it.

'He's very nurturing,' Billie notices.

Their rapport, they both know, is good for Martina.

Billie, chubbier now at forty-five than in the days when she strode so springily on to Centre Court, would be the first to admit she has a slight weight problem. But she still looks good, the wrinkles softened by a cushion of subcutaneous fat.

Martina looks leaner and meaner, like a tennis champion should. She is not the first player to work out seriously with weights, that was Margaret Court, but Martina has muscles and an aerobic capacity to brag about even though she is past her prime, and the most prominent veins in sport, those of her left forearm, are still there bulging. Unfortunately, Martina is

23

an inch shorter and thirteen years older than the reigning Wimbledon champion Steffi Graf. Height is an advantage in tennis. So is youth.

'Why do you play tennis?' Billie Jean King asks.

Martina usually has an answer, a quick retort for everything. Not now.

'Why are you playing tennis? You don't have to.'

Martina really can't answer the question.

'That's what you've got to figure out first,' Billie says, 'because usually the response is very, very quick' – she snaps her chubby fingers – 'it's like a reaction, not even a response.' Most people play because they love tennis. If Martina has lost her love of tennis, she had better find it soon. 'Otherwise you're not gonna be playing well and you should just quit. You don't wanta play.'

Martina is pretty close to giving up. 'It was at Amelia Island that I hit rock bottom. It was really frustrating.' But deep down she does want to play. She has more outside interests than most tennis players, but she is not ready yet to be an ex-tennis player.

'All right,' Billie says. 'Pretend Craig and I are ten years old and we've never played tennis, and you're gonna teach us.'

'You're my coaches,' Martina says. 'I'm paying you to coach me.'

'Well, guess what, this is lesson one, this is what we're gonna do because we feel we've gotta know what you know about the sport, and what you don't know about it, what your thoughts are on technique, and the game and the face of the racket. And let's go.'

But as she tries to explain to Billie and Craig and therefore to herself the basics of the game with which she has had the longest, most passionate, the deepest relationship of her life, Martina is floundering.

'She was very stymied,' recalls Billie Jean King. 'She was lost when she was telling Craig and me. She was just floundering.' As to why she was playing, 'She didn't know.'

'You know how bad it got?' Martina could explain just a month later. 'My technique was so bad that I had to stop and think

24

about every shot. Was my shoulder turning the right way? What should I do next? How should I even hit the ball? It was not that I didn't know what to do but I wasn't sure actually how to do it. Basic. After all those years. I was tired of playing and not enjoying it even when I won.' As usual Judy's questions had helped Martina find the answer: call Billie. Martina's talk with Judy had rebonded their 'marriage', which had some problems.

Martina could still remember the obsessive love of tennis that she had harnessed to become world number one. But she didn't feel it any more. Her tennis was crucial to her life, the core of her existence, and yet somehow she was divorced from it internally. Her motivation, as convoluted as anyone else's — yearnings for freedom, money, applause, acceptance, excellence, power — had been based in her pleasure in and love of tennis. Now that was missing. Yet her desire for a permanent place in tennis history was still there, as insistent as the pain in her knees.

Lesson one — Hey, woman, better realize you're suffering from burn-out — had stung Martina like a jolt of electricity. 'I didn't even know that I had the problem.' Lesson two would provide the current to stimulate her out of the slump. Because of the startling nature of these first sessions and because they gave Martina a spurt of energy, very soon she and Billie would begin to refer to their sessions together as jolts.

Lesson two begins. 'Go back to when you were a child, Martina, and first started to play tennis.' Martina had fallen deeply and instinctively in love with tennis as a child. If she can find that initial joy, it is likely she can conquer burn-out. 'So take us back to your beginnings playing tennis in Czechoslovakia. Tell me how it felt, what the smells were, all your senses.'

She smelled the clay, the burnt, terracotta-coloured crushed clay of the tennis court. She smelled the freshness after it had rained. She loved playing at the club, her grandmother had played there and her mother. The skinny little girl with the cropped brown hair, who had been given a racket by her grandmother when she was just four and a half years old, used to spend hours hitting balls against her favourite wall in the village of Revnice where she grew up, 27 kilometres south of Prague. Sometimes there were wheelbarrows of red clay near the courts. Sometimes, your feet left a bright red trail.

'I don't remember the exact day or moment when I felt the racket for the first time,' Martina says, 'but I remember having to hold it with both hands. It was an old wooden racket from my grandmother with a wooden handle, no leather grips. I just hit two-handed backhands against the wall.'

All children play pretend games. Martina imagined she was playing against great champions when she hit balls against her favourite wall. 'In my head, I was playing Rod Laver.' Or she was Rod Laver or Rosie Casals or Billie Jean King. At the age of nine, Martina saw her first Wimbledon on television. It didn't matter if the picture was fuzzy. 'I remember watching Billie Jean win, that was in sixty-six. I thought I could do it one day. I don't know why.' Long before she was that grown up, long before she had a racket, in fact while she was still a baby, tennis had entered Martina's life as an object of longing.

You could see a tennis court from the room in which Martina, an only child, lived with her mother. Martina was told that her grandparents who lived in a room upstairs had once owned the whole house and the tennis court opposite. Both now belonged to the Czech state. There were several families living in the big, increasingly decrepit house. The tennis court, no longer in use, was deteriorating. From time to time, Martina climbed into the apple orchard which she was told had once belonged to her family, and stole apples.

From the point of view of the government, appropriating the property had been a matter of sharing the wealth, on the Marxist principle of from each according to their ability, to each according to their need. To the family, it felt like injustice, the

26

theft of young Martina's birthright. All that the family had left was outrage and a sense of displacement in their own country. The little girl Martina inherited both. They would prove to be valuable heirlooms.

So would the family's one great intangible heirloom, its sporting tradition, which no government could appropriate. Tennis had entered the family through the female line. Martina's grandmother Agnes Semanska had at one time been ranked as the Czech number five. Her most notable victory, one the family still talked about, was a triumph over Vera Sukova's mother in the national championships. Vera Sukova was the first Czech woman ever to reach a Wimbledon final. Agnes Semanska's glory was at one remove. Perhaps her granddaughter would do better.

Martina started tennis with a great disadvantage. Unlike Chris Evert, Martina did not have a professional tennis coach for a father. In fact, she lacked a father altogether. Her parents separated when she was three. Martina remembers being with her father when she was four, at a ski lodge where there were lots of dogs, collies. There was the occasional visit to the zoo, but when she was seven or eight, she lost track of him. 'People say that my wild swings of mood, the gush of tears after a loss, the giddy exuberance when I was on a roll during the early years of my tennis career, were like my father.'

Her mother Jana, long-limbed, strong and agile, Agnes Semanska's daughter, loved sports too. Jana was a ski instructor in the Krkonose mountains when she met her first husband Miroslav Subert, who was working for the ski patrol. It was not surprising that their child Martina was gifted athletically. Named after Martinovka, the ski lodge where she had been conceived, Martina Subertova was born on 18 October 1956 in Prague, where her mother had gone for the delivery. In Czech, Subertova is the feminine version of Subert.

At two, Martina was already learning to ski in the Krkonose, but when her parents' marriage broke down, she moved with her mother to the family home in the village of Revnice. Martina the toddler had probably already absorbed the lesson Jana was teaching by example, that 'sports are good for young women'. It was good to run, to sweat, to compete and feel tired, healthy and refreshed.

Martina was three and a half when she met Miroslav Navratil who would become her first coach. It was a tradition at the local tennis club for everyone to help with the upkeep, and Miroslav was pushing a wheelbarrow that he had just emptied of red clay. Martina, the family story goes, hitched a ride in the wheelbarrow. It would be two years before he became her coach. First he became her stepfather. Miroslav, who had the same first name as her father, was known by his nickname Mirek. Jana and Mirek were married on 1 July 1961, after Jana's divorce. The stepfather moved in with Martina and her mother. Both took his name, the feminine version being Navratilova. Two years later, when Martina was almost seven, her half-sister Jana was born, eventually meriting them a second room in the house.

Miroslav Navratil, an adequate club player, recognized that Martina had real talent and promised her that one day she would be a champion. To help her, he became a devoted and a demanding coach. 'If he had a dollar for every hour he spent with me,' she said, 'he'd be a millionaire. He loved me so much.'

That part wasn't difficult. 'I was always smiling, I hardly ever cried. I was a real sweetie.'

Some people say he quickly lost the upper hand with his wife and the child was the only one who would do his bidding. But it doesn't really matter whether or not he directed the child because he couldn't control the mother. He did a good job. That we know.

The neighbours remember the petite grandmother Agnes Semanska with great pleasure. They also remember the young Martina fondly. She was the little girl who ran to get stronger with what seemed to be bricks in her rucksack. Mainly she got into shape, Martina says, by running for the train to Prague for tennis practice. She was always in such a hurry that she would have to go straight from school carrying her heavy bag full of books and tennis gear. One of her grandmother's old friends, though, is sure she remembers Martina running with a rucksack filled with bricks. It is quite a good method. Another says she saw Martina cry when her parents refused to let her go skiing because she might break an ankle or leg and that would ruin her for tennis. Skiing was a big sport in Revnice.

Martina now lives in Colorado snow country where she can ski from her front door. As an adult she has skied despite the dangers, even skied uninsured, which is unusual for a professional athlete. She said the premium was too high but maybe another reason was that she wanted the luxury of living dangerously.

In Revnice it is thought by some that Miroslav Navratil made a Faustian bargain on his stepdaughter's behalf. The legendary Faust is said to have lived in Prague. To this day there is a house in the city which tourist guides point out as his. Faust promised his soul to the devil in exchange for the particular sort of success he wanted in life. Martina's stepfather promised her tennis success. The cost was not her soul. It was, say some of the neighbours, her childhood. Perhaps they are merely envious.

By train from Prague, it is only a short trip to Revnice.

— 2 —

Closely Watched Trains

Buttoning on his shirt, Miroslav Navratil answers the ring of the door bell. As the door opens I can see his naked chest and stomach. 'Yes,' he calls in Czech, standing in the doorway, buttoning up the shirt. The front door is at the top of a long flight of stairs, well away from the gate. The door bell is in the gate.

'*Ahoj*,' I call up to him. In Czech that's hello; it sounds like 'Ahoy'. 'I am a journalist and I want to talk to you about Martina, about the days when you were coaching her in her childhood.'

A look of pleasure comes over his face. 'Wait,' he says, 'I'll ask my wife.'

I gulp. My Czech friend Hana has already spoken to his wife. Only an hour ago, as I sat drinking the Czech aperitif Becherovka at Hana's kitchen table, she telephoned requesting an interview for the lady from the *Sunday Times*. I am in Prague to attend the April 1994 European Tennis Congress and I want to visit the scenes of Martina's early life. The conversation in Czech between Hana and Mrs Navratilova had been terribly brief.

'*Pani* Navratilova was brusque,' Hana said. *Pani* is Mrs in Czech. 'She says they are leaving immediately for a holiday, and will be away for ten days.'

30

'Oh well,' I said, pouring us each another Becherovka. 'It's one of those things.' I had not liked the idea of going to see them before I mentioned the book to Martina, whom I had been trying to reach through her agent for over a month.

'I think we must go immediately to Revnice,' says Hana, my easy-going, good-natured, assistant interpreter. Her day job is as a PE teacher.

'She is under no obligation to see us.'

'*Pani* should be polite. She is Czech.'

Marou, a professional interpreter who soon joins us at the kitchen table, is also surprised that we have not been invited to visit them.

'They probably get many requests,' I say. 'They have a right to say no.'

'Come,' says Hana. 'We go.'

'*Ano, ano, ano,*' says Marou. This means yes, yes, yes.

Vera, Hana's 85-year-old mother whose homemade prune cake we are eating with the Becherovka, and who has been following the conversation with simultaneous interpretation, nods encouragement to me. Czech civilization, I am beginning to feel, is at stake. I down my Becherovka and, against my better judgement, we run for the tram. Roger Bannister, the man who made the decision to attempt the world's first four-minute mile despite a head wind and succeeded, said, 'Sport, like all life, is about taking your chances,' but I am not eager today to tempt fate.

The tram passes Klamovka Park where the young Martina played tennis on the first indoor court in Prague, and takes us to the Metro. It is just one stop on the B line to Smichov station where we will catch the train to Revnice. It is Friday evening and the weather is good. No doubt there will be a long queue. This is not the way I like to travel, not the way I like to do business either. 'We should have an appointment,' I say. 'It is not polite to barge in.'

'It is she who is impolite,' say the two Czechs, Hana and Marou, in one voice. I know they are wrong; but I go anyway.

The ticket queue at the train station puts one in mind of a South African polling station. 'We're going to miss the train,' I say, with relief.

Rummaging in her purse, in Marou's purse and in mine, Hana finds enough coins, plucks me from the queue, and leads the way to the automatic ticket machine which accepts eight *koruna*, 19 pence, from each of us, and spits out a yellow ticket for the 26-minute journey to the village of Revnice. We board the ancient, graffiti-smeared train. Instead of the usual scrawled male organs, the graffiti are of female genitalia. There are no penises in Czech graffiti, Marou explains, only stylized cunts. Some folklorists and ethnologists believe, she says, that this gives a deep insight into the Czech character. There are more graffiti now than when the Communists were in charge, but there would have been graffiti on the trains when nine-year-old Martina was riding in to Prague for tennis lessons at Klamovka and then to play among the chosen at Sparta tennis club.

The trains run on time. Twenty-six minutes later we enter Revnice, the Nazareth of Navratilovity. A middle-aged man on a bicycle with a tennis racket sticking out of his rucksack hurries by, and there is a twelve- or thirteen-year-old girl in pigtails carrying a tennis racket. 'Look,' says Hana, 'she could be Martina as a child. Everyone here plays tennis.'

'No,' the neighbours would tell us, she never had a ponytail or pigtails. For as far back as anyone can remember, with her cropped hair, long legs and boy's shirts, the young Martina looked like a boy. This in itself is not unusual. Many pre-pubescent girls have physiques that we consider to be boyish. Many grown women do too. Thus, their bodies are not really boyish, except by convention.

What is less usual is that Martina seems always to have been dressed as a boy. Odd in the matriarchy that Mirek Navratil married into, in which sporting talent had been handed down along the female line.

People direct us to the new house in Marakova street, at the top of the village, which is a mixture of picturesque old and

32

ugly new buildings, with a sprinkling of agreeable modern houses. The Navratils' is one of them. At first we assume that the house with the big satellite dish must be theirs. With satellite they can see Martina play no matter where she is when she is abroad. Their house turns out to be the one across the street. The lane is unpaved. Two houses away, a woman and her son are transplanting raspberries.

Now as Martina's stepfather, his shirttails flying, three buttons done up, vanishes behind the wooden trim of the front door, I'm wondering if this was a good idea. Instantly his wife Jana appears at the top of the stairs. I do a double take. It could be Martina twenty years from now. Like her daughter, Jana Navratilova is a handsome woman, tall, athletic, good bones. She has on a bulky pale cardigan that says Wimbledon on it.

'*Ahoj*,' I call to her. '*Ahoj*. Hello.'

'What do you want?'

'To say hello.'

'We have no time, we have people coming for a party.' Her English is good.

'I'm sorry to intrude. Really.' Really, I am. I have never doorstepped anyone before in my life. My Czech friends look at me reproachfully. 'May I just ask you one thing, how were you able to realize so young that Martina had talent? We want to know how you and your husband saw it in her.'

'We have people coming for a party.'

My Czech friends look at her reproachfully.

'I understand. We should have an appointment.'

Jana Navratilova comes down the flight of steps to the gate. 'She was very eager to play tennis, and we liked it too. It was not a talent we had, it was her, we didn't have to push her, she wanted to play.'

'That was when you lived in that house across the street from the old tennis court.'

'Yes, 108 Prazska.' She seems about to say more, but thinks better of it. Visiting her daughter at Wimbledon, Jana Navratilova has come up against the best doorsteppers in the world,

33

the men from the *News of the World* and the *Sun*. That surely is why the gate is so high and the front door has been placed at a defensive height. As I say good-bye, she seems surprised at my lack of persistence. 'It's that way,' she says, pointing down the hill toward Prazska Street. Through the barrier of the front gate she shakes my hand.

I am astonished at her courtesy.

My Czech companions are less impressed. 'Here you can drop in even on strangers,' Hana says. 'And how could they be going away immediately if they were also having a party?'

'It was a good touch. She made it clear that she was choosing not to see us, which was her right.'

A couple of houses down the unpaved lane, the neighbour who was planting raspberries with her son invites us in to look at the garden and chat. 'Ah, mahonia,' Hana says, examining the scratchy red and green leaves and the scant yellow blossoms. I recognize the forsythia which is also in yellow flower. Something two-legged races across my path.

'Roosters,' I exclaim in English.

'He does not like them,' the neighbour Vera Novakova points to the Navratil house and says with relish. 'He says they crow too early. These are new ones I got very recently. We will see how he adapts to them.' We are not allowed to leave without drinking coffee and accepting some seeds of a plant none of us recognizes and, for the foreigner, a tiny vase as a souvenir.

Like its identical neighbours, 108 Prazska, the house beside the railway track that Martina grew up in, is an ungainly block of a building, faced with cracked and chipping concrete. It is one of those squarish houses, most of them built between the wars, that blight the Czech landscape. In the gloomy outlying districts of Prague itself and in nearby villages, far from the famously beautiful architecture of early Prague, there are too many of these monstrosities. The house is, as Martina remembered it from exile and her ghostwriter described it in the autobiography, large enough to turn into flats. But surely it was never what the classified ads would call a 'des res' (desirable residence).

Martina, like any village child, sometimes watched the trains go by. The tracks run behind the backyard of the house. The train to Prague passes many times a day. At the station, just a few minutes' walk away, the trains come to a spluttering stop and start until late. The dusty factory opposite the station has always employed many people in the town.

People who live near trains often yearn to travel. It occurs to them early that you can live somewhere else. Even the name of the street encouraged Martina to think of a world bigger than Revnice. Prazska is Czech for Prague Street.

They still do not understand capitalism properly in Revnice. In the village, anyone can tell you which was the house of Martina Navratilova's childhood and where her parents live now. But there are no signs, no banners, no little plaques on the house to commemorate Revnice's most famous daughter. The tennis court Martina gazed at through the window has all but disappeared to neglect. If you squint, you can just make out the rusty remnants of the posts which supported the net all those years ago. If this were a town in her adopted country, there would be neon signs directing you to the original tennis court, to her first tennis club, to the lost apple trees.

It is easy to sneer at the possibility of neon, and certainly there is something endearing about the commercial innocence of Revnice, although with the galloping economic changes in the Czech Republic innocence may be debauched all too soon. But a discreet sign would not be amiss. Someone ought to mark the monuments.

Martina's parents ceded 108 Prazska to a relative when they thought they were escaping to a new life in the America of the 1980s. Unhappy with what they found there, they returned and have a better house now. Fortunately, Martina had money enough to buy them another and she was generous enough to want to do so.

A woman who worked under Miroslav at the factory, where he was a kind of foreman, thinks he may have been henpecked at home. Perhaps that was why he seemed to enjoy telling those under him and the child Martina what to do. Aside from Martina herself, the only other serious tennis player, the grandmother Agnes Semanska, seems to have been well loved in that village. Although not everyone in the village speaks fondly of Martina's parents, it is clear that they wanted the best for her.

Miroslav Navratil, whom Martina thought of as her father, seems to have been a devoted one. Martina's childhood, as one reads of it in her autobiography, was close to idyllic. Tolstoy was wrong when he said happy families are all alike. Each family is informed by its own motif. The Navratils suffered from the standard Czech social schizophrenia. It was a craziness not in themselves but in their stars, caused by the politics of the country. The ideology was, don't support the system, avoid it. Theirs was the family against the world, and for each other; a stepfather who recognized her talent and worked to develop it; a mother who being sporty herself did not limit her daughter; two doting grandmothers always near. To be sure there was a difficult grandfather now dead. There was even a younger sister to dominate. And above all there was tennis, a sport in which everyone recognized very early on that she was gifted.

At four and a half, little Marti began hitting against a cement wall with that old, hand-me-down racket which was slightly crooked at the head. As she got older, Miroslav encouraged her, 'Pretend you're at Wimbledon.' He had promised her she would be a champion and entered her in her first tournament at eight. Martina's first taste of triumph, when she won the under-10s and the under-12s, was a pleasure they shared. Many people remember them arriving at tournaments on Mirek's motorcycle, Martina laden with tennis rackets and clinging to his back.

The Czech Republic is a tiny country. Drive two hours in any direction and you are in another land, Poland to the north,

Austria if you go south, and to the west, Germany. All of these countries are many times bigger than the Republic yet only massive Germany has had as many tennis champions. It is not anything mysterious in the water. Rather, for generations tennis has been one of the big sports in the Republic and Czech bureaucrats fought hard to convince the Communist regime, which usually backed only Olympic sport, to back tennis in Czechoslovakia.

The Czech version of America's Nick Bollettieri tennis academy was of as high quality but infinitely more low key. Instead of moving in, players who were accepted for coaching came after school. This wasn't simply a matter of paying for it. For this you had to qualify and, in what was a crucial revision of the standard communist doctrine, the Czech Tennis Federation offered training *to* each according to ability, providing not lavishly, but well. The training programme had a bit in common with the public parks systems that existed on a smaller scale in America and gave us Wimbledon champions Althea Gibson and Billie Jean King. It is similar to the open, non-class-based system which is struggling to be born in Britain and may by the year 2000 result in champions.

To sail through the Czech system of elite clubs for elite players, however, you needed enthusiastic parents. When her stepfather promised that she would win Wimbledon one day, Martina says, 'I believed him. He didn't tell me I was going to do it nine times, though.'

To fulfil their dream, when she was nine he took her to Prague for a try out with the Czech equivalent of a tennis pro at Klamovka Tennis Club. She passed it. 'I think we can do something with her,' the instructor George Parma said.

Twice a week after school, Martina now took the train to Prague where she boarded the tram that went down busy Plzenska street. Instead of the splendid old city of architectural fame, on the tram ride from Smichov station Martina passed through the seedy Prague of dour reality. Streets of drab brown buildings, many with scaffolding affixed to hold them up, advertised their decades of neglect. For the older generation decrepitude became a symbol of resistance. A state of depression was fairly universal. Everyone was employed, no one worked. Everyone knew how to look busy. 'We pretend we're working,' a Czech ironist quipped, 'and they pretend they're paying us.'

The child Martina understood little of this. But she couldn't miss seeing the decrepitude. As soon as you get off the tram at the stop called Klamovka at the edge of Klamovka park, you have to cross traffic-filled Plzenska street. Martina's other grandmother Andela Subertova, her father's mother, was often there waiting at the tram stop for Martina. They would cross together very carefully, the little old lady in black dress and stockings and the long, lean child. Together they would walk up the hill, past the bus stop and the big forsythia bush, to the tennis courts. Andela Subertova, whom Martina called Babicka – the Czech word for grandmother – lived in a flat virtually in sight of the tennis club. Sometimes she stayed to watch the practice. Babicka was not interested in tennis but her Martinka was her 'golden little girl'.

Martina loved Babicka very much. Long after she had moved to America, Martina had recurring dreams about running and trying to get to Babicka, whom she couldn't reach. 'She's in my dreams,' Martina said, 'more than anybody else.'

After the mid-week session, Babicka usually shepherded Martinka back to the tram, but on Friday nights she stayed over. There was a lesson on Saturday. Martinka and Babicka had a wonderful time doing crosswords and eating suppers of chicken with carrot salad, which Babicka always pointed out was good for your eyes. 'People say grandparents are going out of style. I had the real thing: a little old Czech grandmother who loved me and whose memory keeps me going today.'

The Klamovka Tennis Club, which housed the first indoor courts in Prague in what looked like an aircraft hangar, is not what it has been. It is hard to find now, its light not so much hidden under a bushel as behind a billboard and a car-hire agency. Two men cleaning the interior of one car point me beyond the rental office to what looks like an empty car park. There are puddles in the cracked paving. This is all that remains of the covered tennis courts.

'Seven years ago, it fell down,' explains the grey-haired current director. As the Communists were still in power, it was not rebuilt. It just missed out on the Velvet Revolution.

The outdoor tennis courts beyond, surrounded by trees, are so near the main thoroughfare that you can hear the trams if you listen for them. You don't. Like Sparta, the more elite club Martina would move to later, it is green here, with much foliage. Calm, beautiful. The backboards and the wooden surrounds are painted the dull, dark, elegant green of England and Europe. Few American courts are painted this traditional colour. On a cold, damp afternoon, the courts are deserted, but they are well maintained, the clay intact. Even in the gloom of a rainy day, you can imagine the absent players, and almost hear the ball thunk. In this weather, there are only a few players even at the Czech showcase courts on the other side of Prague. George Parma too is long gone. Even before Martina, he went to America.

The new director, Vaclav Bloha, lives in the building beside the court. 'Write only nice things,' he advised, 'because she is a wonderful player and a wonderful woman.' She *is* a hero to the Czech people.

You have to move on when you need to if you are really going somewhere. Sparta, much bigger, and in the midst of giant Stromovka park, was the best club in Prague. Getting there involved a train, a tram, and a two-mile walk uphill. Now, if you go by the back route, there is a bus stop nearby.

The finest male player since Drobny, Jan Kodes, twice French Open champion, was a member of the Sparta Tennis Club, as was his married sister the long-time Czech number one Vlasta Vopickova. Invited to play at Sparta, Martina was soon chosen as Kodes's doubles partner. 'I was a raw player and scared to death of letting down the great Kodes. Yet he trusted me to take my share of shots at the net.'

In fact, from her first appearance on the Czech junior circuit, Martina had made an impression. When the teenaged Martina first walked into the women's changing room, Vlasta Vopicková and the others had gaped. 'We thought a boy had walked in by mistake. Her hair was so short and she was wearing boy's shorts.' In Eastern Europe at that time, dress was not unisex. It is more so these days but even now Vlasta, huskier than Martina, coach at Prague's showplace tennis centre, Stvanice, arrives in high heels and changes into her tracksuit. Wondering if her remark was a Czech way of alluding to Martina's homosexuality, I probed delicately. 'No,' said Vlasta. 'We had no idea that she was interested in girls until we read it in the newspaper. Here she had a boyfriend. People used to say the boy was no good in bed and that is why she turned to girls.' That is one of the things people say. Martina herself said rather undiplomatically in print that the boy was no good. Later, she would talk of the other reasons for her interest in women.

Photographs of Martina show a child who is dressed like a boy. Childhood pictures without ribbons on the girls usually are androgenous, for little girls and little boys look remarkably alike with their clothes on. Chris Evert's father taught her tennis, but afterwards her mother put her in dresses. Martina's, it seems, didn't.

Martina says in her autobiography that she was mistaken for a boy and that sometimes it upset her. She also says that Rita Mae Brown, the American writer with whom she lived for three years and with whom she broke up acrimoniously, believed herself to be a man trapped in a woman's body. 'Everybody seizes on that,' says Rita Mae, 'and it's not true. I think that was her little slap in my face. It's pretty funny.' Her voice rises in amusement. From what I knew of Rita Mae and of her politics, it had seemed unlikely. 'I never thought people would really grab on to it the way they did, but that again is very political, it's a very negative view of lesbianism. I was the kind of girl that dressed up in my mother's clothes. I was one of those.'

Evidently, Martina wasn't. As a child, the novelist Daphne

du Maurier wanted to be and for a time actually convinced herself that she was a boy. But the wish to be physically male is not a common phenomenon, even among women who are lesbian. Penis envy has to do with power rather than parts. Martina has said publicly and told me that she did not know she was lesbian until she was eighteen, but, as I will explain later, Billie Jean King seems to have had a different impression from Martina, who understandably might have discussed her sexuality more informally with a friend. Even if she did know earlier, that wouldn't necessarily have anything to do with boyish appearance, despite the stereotypes.

Did Martina, I asked Rita Mae Brown, want to be or think she was a boy? 'Well, look, she never said anything to me. I don't know if it ever crossed her mind. She didn't look like a boy to me, I just thought she looked like a very athletic, healthy person, like a real healthy kind of outdoorsy woman. I don't like people that look, you know, phony. She looked real natural to me. She still does. I think she's a real interesting looking person.'

'Of course life has changed her,' Vlasta says approvingly. 'She dresses up now, wears earrings, and she doesn't walk like a boy. She now uses make-up, takes care of herself – not like when she was fourteen.'

'I was comfortable how I was,' says Martina. 'I wanted to wear shorts, I wanted to have short hair, I thought it was cool to be an athlete. I wouldn't have changed places with another girl for anything in the world.' There were moments, though, when 'I thought I looked too much like a boy and I wasn't ever gonna be, you know, pretty and that the boys weren't going to like me. Little did I know I wouldn't care later on if they did or not.'

Martina was accepted at Sparta for what she was, an excellent player. 'She came to the net. She would throw herself at the net,' recalls Vlasta, 'and other women were afraid.'

Vlasta's brother Jan, who needed a partner for the mixed doubles, urged her forward. 'I could see she had the talent so I encouraged her,' recalled Jan Kodes, now greying but still wiry and agile. In tennis, Czech society is entirely egalitarian in one respect. People think women should play with the same vigour and aggression as men.

Everywhere the moment comes when the promising young player has to demonstrate her power by overwhelming the old champion. The match for the national championship was between Martina and Vlasta Vopickova who had been the Czech number one for most of a decade. The place was called Ostrava. Martina remembers it well. It was the summer before her sixteenth birthday, 1972, and Martina, the underdog, had flu. 'I probably should have defaulted earlier in the tournament.' She kept going during the final by sipping hot tea. Going for a low shot she scraped her right knee painfully.

As it happened, all seven times Vlasta had played in Ostrava she had lost, which was odd because she was a winner. 'But everyone told me I didn't have to worry this time because I was playing a youngster. "This is going to break your streak of bad luck, here, Vlasta. She won't be a match for you."' Vlasta had had her first child six months earlier and wanted to retire as the title holder. She had always beaten Martina and wouldn't have worried except she was out of condition and it was Ostrava.

The day was hot. Flu or no, Martina needed to prove to herself that she was a real champion. She came out on court and immediately attacked. 'That extraordinary slicing backhand, that was very disagreeable,' recalls Vlasta. The match was hard fought, Vlasta believing she could finally win here, Martina knowing that it was she who must. The final score, which both remember, was 7–5, 6–2, and Martina won.

The match that elevated her to Czech number two was a rite of passage. 'It meant I was good enough to play on the international circuit.'

To Vlasta too, that day in Ostrava signalled something more than defeat. 'I never beat her any more. And we all knew then she would be a great champion.'

*   *   *

When the Communists were in control, few Czechs could travel, and those who could – ice-hockey players, tennis players and diplomats – were subject to constant indignities. The gargantuan Communist party headquarters near the river, close to the centre of Prague, was the seat of power. Bureaucrats there spent their days refusing other Czechs *vystupni viza*, exit visas. In a country which has used its sense of irony as a tool of survival, it is not surprising that soon after the Velvet Revolution the Communist party headquarters was turned into the Ministry of Travel. When I asked the press officer of the Czech Tennis Federation which was the Communist party headquarters, he smiled gleefully and ran outside in his shirt sleeves in wet, blustery weather to show me, and said, 'Now we go where we want.'

It is hard to imagine what life was like in a society where ideology had long since overruled compassion and even common sense. Czech farmers' sons were even sent to work in the city lest they become too attached to the newly collectivized farms. Czechoslovakia never suffered severely from lack of food. What it lacked was purpose and hope, spelled out by those unpainted muddy brown façades and the cracked concrete floors of the tenement buildings built between the wars. Today Prague is tarted up, painted like the expensive whore it is becoming as it lures Western bankers and corporate executives.

Life everywhere in the Soviet bloc had been an illustration of 'how metaphysics in one man's head can turn into shit on another's head'. All over the Soviet Union walls were decked with Red banners proclaiming Communist slogans that were moronic as well as immoral: 'The party is the mind, the honour and the conscience of our epoch.' People were frightened in Moscow, hungry in Lithuania, and cowed in Czechoslovakia. No one did anything they weren't told to do and if they had any esprit, they hid it. Only on the court could one dream.

In the old days it had been even worse. Jaroslav Drobny was regularly body-searched as he departed for Wimbledon. 'They

43

made me strip and they even checked my socks, the ones I was wearing.'

When he defected in 1949, it was not smooth sailing. He attempted to become Australian, British, American or the citizen of some smaller European haven or even a Caribbean island. Finally, when no one else would take him, Drobny became the first Egyptian player of top rank. Five years after his defection, he married an Englishwoman, and began to raise a family. Five years after his marriage, as was the law at the time, he was granted British citizenship.

The Czechs knew this edifying story of defection followed by difficulty. The Czech Tennis Federation had a habit of sending players off without enough money to pay for both food and lodging and young men who would not otherwise have eaten breakfast on the morning of a tournament sometimes slept on Drobny's sofa. 'I got calls from the airport,' recalls Drobny, 'and sometimes when they had no money to get into town, I drove over to Heathrow to meet them.'

There had been two great waves of defection: Drobny's the year following 1948 when the Russians first occupied the country, and another after the spring of 1968, when the Russian tanks arrived again to clamp down on their straying satellite. For the Czech people, who had been experiencing the freer policies of the Dubcek government known as the Prague Spring, and who had thought that communism would now have a more human face, the arrival of Russian tanks was a disaster. To twelve-year-old Martina Navratilova it was an exciting moment when her stepfather arrived on his motorcycle to take her home. They passed tanks in the streets and saw them on the roads as they travelled the miles from Pilsen to Revnice. That day, in which Martina was too young to participate, would, like the Houston caucus of nine angry female tennis players two years later, which she also did not attend, vastly affect Martina's life. 'My happy life in Czechoslovakia changed drastically when the Communists took over in 1968.' In fact, the Communists had already been there for two decades and Martina's life was not immediately affected, but the frosting over of the Prague Spring meant that Martina, the individualist, would have to go elsewhere if she wanted to shine.

The victory over Vlasta opened the door to Wimbledon but for some time Martina had been travelling abroad on the junior circuit. Her first trip had been to West Germany. She liked what she knew of the West.

'Whenever she got out, she would be like a fish in water,' recalled Vlasta. 'We were scared. We didn't feel secure abroad, we were homesick. But she thrived. It was evident.' Her tennis was thriving too, and it was becoming evident to the national coach Vera Sukova that Martina was an exceptionally gifted player.

Sukova, whose mother had been defeated by Martina's grandmother, had been a Wimbledon finalist in 1962. Her young daughter Helena would also become a distinguished tennis player. Vera herself was in charge of the Czech juniors. Martina travelled to Eastern Europe regularly now with Vera Sukova and the team for competition. Finally there were visits to the West. The former British player Shirley Brasher who had known Vera Sukova in their playing days, remembers being buttonholed by Vera at a women's under-21 international team competition in France. Vera, who knew her tennis, had realized early on that the Czechs had a potential champion in Martina.

'You must look at her, we have hope for her,' Vera Sukova told Shirley Brasher.

— 3 —

You Can't Go Home Again

The sun rises high above the irrigated palm trees. Blue skies. Green lawns. Black men painting the white houses whiter. The silence is broken by the serpentine hiss of a gargantuan sprinkler system striking. Florida on a winter's day in 1973. To Martina, sixteen years old, on her first visit to the land of Evert, the sunshine in March, the open skies and open faces, are astonishing. Everything looks so new. For many of the Americans she has met since she arrived, and whom she will meet in the next days and months, it would be impossible even to imagine how down at the heel Eastern Europe is, how dreary, especially on a winter's day. With the sun in her eyes – perhaps blinding her to defects? – Martina sets out on this March day to explore the land of the free and the home of the brave. From the first, her America is a land of tennis whites.

What is the cultural centre of this universe? The Seven-Eleven store? The tennis court?

At Seven-Eleven, you might see a guy busily stacking groceries on to shelves already crowded. No shortages and a clerk actually working. At home, where the Czechs hate the communist bosses, the art of expending the minimum amount of energy with the maximum flourish has been well developed. The illusion had been going on for a quarter of a century. Prices were high, stocks were low, and you didn't learn to work the system,

46

you learned to work outside of it. Here at the Seven-Eleven, there's plenty to buy and no queue at all. Martina won't have to scrimp and save on this trip. Or starve herself. Here there will be plenty of money for food *and* souvenirs. What a country. The streets are paved with groceries.

To her, at that moment, Florida is most certainly not the land of the bland. It is neither too hot, too humid, nor too flat, and it doesn't occur to her that it may be soulless. What it is to her is an antidote to drab, dull, unpainted, unloved Prague and Revnice. And how do they keep it so bright, so clean?

Even more than the Seven-Eleven, perhaps, Martina admires the all-American style of the Fort Lauderdale Tennis Club. Look at that blonde teenager over by the clubhouse. Just two years older than Martina but already famous. Chris Evert is instantly recognizable from the pages of *World Tennis* which, with the help of a dictionary, Martina has been reading for a couple of years now. In 1971, three months before her seventeenth birthday, Chris became the youngest player ever to reach the semi-finals of the US Open, where she lost to Billie Jean King because, Chris says, she got her first period just a few days before the match. She didn't even know it was a period, thought the blood stain came from a scratch or something. Martina's was a shock to her too when it came at age fourteen. The birds and the bees can be a mystery to budding tennis champions.

The following season, Chris made it to the semi-finals of Wimbledon – Martina's court of dreams – and the US Open. For Chris Evert, who had played seriously as an amateur and had only become a professional on 21 December 1972, her eighteenth birthday, grand slam victories seem to be just around the corner.

Tennis is not yet a teenager's paradise. The big names are the thirty-year-old 1973 world number one Margaret Court, and the number two Billie Jean King, twenty-nine. Virginia Wade, her best ranking still in the future, is twenty-seven. The only precocious teenager is Chris Evert, America's Sweetheart –

except to those who believe a girl should show tears or elation on court, to whom she is the Ice Maiden.

Chris, who is blonde and can pass for beautiful, is coolly whiling away half an hour playing backgammon – Martina's eyes zero in on the red and black board. Backgammon pieces look like checkers, but the game is very different. Checkers is amiable; backgammon is more aggressive.

Chris is playing against some guy, who, Martina soon learns, is the tournament referee. Chris's sister Jean, who plays tennis too, is also there. Chris seems very much at home. She should. Fort Lauderdale is her home. She grew up at this club where her father was the tennis pro. It is her turn now. With the same concentration that would carry her to the finals at both Wimbledon and the French Open, Chris throws the dice. She gazes deeply at the backgammon board. Then she makes her move. If you're a good player you're thinking points ahead, just as you do on a tennis court. The elements of chance and skill are nicely balanced in both games. Chris doesn't even look up until Martina and her Czech companion are quite close. The other Czech who played the circuit last year calls out, 'Hi.'

Chris Evert removes her gaze from the board and returns the greeting. Seeing Martina, whom she has never met, she nods politely. Martina, just two years younger, who could easily reach out and touch Chris if she wanted to, is very much aware of the professional distance between them. Just being acknowledged by Chris, Martina will say later, gives her goosebumps. Chris represents everything Martina yearns for. 'Before I met her, she stood for everything I admired in this country: poise, ability, sportsmanship, money, style.' Martina still remembers the moment: 'I can remember it like it was yesterday.'

But the moment didn't register with Chris who was used to awed newcomers.

Their second meeting, but their first on a tennis court, was later that month, at a tournament in Akron, Ohio. The female vocalist of The Pretenders, Chrissie Hynde, was born in Akron, but in 1973, The Pretenders weren't famous yet. Other than that, this city in the American middle west was hardly a place of note or fable. At the tournament, Martina had the ill fortune of drawing Chris in the first round. Instead of feeling hopelessness, disappointment and dread, Martina says she was 'thrilled to death' at the prospect of competing against Chris. Perhaps. In any event, Martina most certainly was not intimidated and before a crowd of a few hundred, on 22 March 1973, she battled to a very honourable defeat, Chris winning 7–6, 6–3. To take someone of Chris's stature to a tie-break – which Chris won at 5–4 to take the first set – was something to write home about.

Chris herself was impressed. 'I'd never heard of her or seen her play, so I was shocked by her big serve, which was probably one of the best, even at that young age. I also noticed she was very emotional and vocal – she whined a lot on court.'

The Ohio crowd of a few hundred had no idea they had witnessed the first thrust in a duel that would go on until Chris retired sixteen years later. The competition would be beautifully classic: the emotional, erratic, left-handed serve and volleyer versus a cool, consistent, right-handed baseliner. Martina was physically stronger and more muscular and her game had more finesse. But Chris could axe you with her two-handed backhand. At the end of the match, she would flash a smile that said, Nothing Personal. That first set tie-break, though no one in the crowd suspected it yet, was the herald of a revolution, the shot that would be heard round the tennis world. Neither Martina nor Chris realized either that the gauntlet had been thrown down and the duel would endure for eighty matches. It was the quiet start of the greatest rivalry in tennis. That includes men's tennis.

Poolside in St Petersburg, Florida, a week or so later, Chris Evert looked up to see a fat girl in a hideous bathing suit sucking a popsicle. She did a double take, and realized with amusement that it was the Czech she had defeated in Akron. Chris remembers this meeting. Not only was the bathing suit terrible, it was too tight, and Martina had strap marks marring her tan. Chris was impressed. She had guts, Chris thought, to go around like that.

Martina didn't appear to realize that the strap marks were less than the height of Florida chic. In any event she couldn't have cared less, she was happy in the sun, happily becoming acclimatized to the tennis life. Although the chlorinated shores of Florida were light years from Martina's background, unfashionable Revnice, they were, she seemed already to have partly sensed, her future. Under the Florida sun, which like Chrissie is pretty consistent, or relentless, depending on your point of view, Martina sucked on the cooling popsicle. Chris would soon be her doubles partner and her friend. This time, it wasn't a matter of goosebumps.

In the baking heat, Martina faced down a six-foot-tall German soon to vanish from the tennis scene. It was now the third week of April. The St Pete tournament was being held in Barlett Park, a public recreation area in a neighbourhood of neat lawns, small retirement homes, and the omnipresent Florida motels. Martina faced Chris on court for the second time in the semifinal. Chris won again. That would be the story for a long time.

It was partly her lack of stamina in the second set that was letting the overweight Martina down. 'The great wide hope' they would soon be calling her. In eight weeks she put on close to 25 pounds. But she was content. She was one of them now, an international tennis player. And all the officials in Czechoslovakia could huff and they could puff but they couldn't make her do everything they wanted her to. Individualism was beckoning. This was a country in which people did what *they* wanted if they could afford it. And if she wanted to she could sit here all day long, licking popsicles until the reddish glow of the sun sank behind the irrigated palm trees.

Meanwhile, all hell was breaking loose in the world of women's tennis. It had come to a head three years earlier, in September 1970, when nine angry women, talking late into the night over spaghetti in a bedroom of a house in Houston, Texas, made the decision that would eventually make Martina Navratilova a millionaire. Neither she, who at the time was a few weeks shy of her fourteenth birthday, nor any of the nine attending the Bedroom Caucus realized that Martina would be the player to benefit most from their decision to form the first all-women tennis tour.

Fed up with the tennis establishment who thought it perfectly right that the prize money for male players was eight times what women were getting – and often more – the women broke permanently with the mixed tour and struck out on their own. Their motive was money not politics. In a sense, though, it was politics: politics is about power. Whereas feminists were arguing that the personal was political and therefore trying to change the drudgery of women's daily lives, the nine understood that money talked. Their actions would lead to a huge influx of money into women's tennis. Twenty-one years later, Martina would retire with twenty million dollars in prize money still atop of what the WTA calls the Money List.

In Martina's first year on the circuit, the birth pains of a player-controlled, professional Open tennis would permeate everything. For one thing, it would delay her first meeting with Billie Jean King. King and the other breakaways were playing on what would become the dominant Virginia Slims women's tour. The Czech Federation had entered Martina in the old official tour. There were a number of other players – including Chris Evert and Virginia Wade – who would take their time deciding to join the breakaways. At first the twain did not often meet except at the four grand slam tournaments – the Australian, French and US Opens and Wimbledon.

That June, 1973, at the French Open, Martina had her biggest win ever, triumphing over Chris Evert's scourge, Nancy Richey, in the third round. To Martina, beating Richey verged on the magical. 'I remember watching Wimbledon on TV in Prague in the early seventies and noticing Billie Jean's serve-and-forehand approach and the fact her contemporary Nancy Richey played in shorts and a hat.' Richey, a Texan, had long been in the top ten in the world rankings. Martina was elated to have defeated her first television personage, and on clay, which was Richey's best surface – and, as it would turn out, Martina's worst.

After that victory, Martina ran into Margaret Court in the locker room. Court said hello, which was nice. It was also surprising because the tall, athletic Australian who hit the hardest ball in the women's game could only have been feeling rotten.

The winner of three Wimbledon and four US Open singles had recently been publicly humiliated in the Battle of the Sexes. This was a ludicrously hyped match played before a television audience of sixty million against Bobbie Riggs, fifty-five, the 1939 Wimbledon champion, now number one in the men's fifty-and-over bracket. Billie Jean King had refused his challenge so he had challenged Margaret Court in order to demonstrate that women weren't equal to men and therefore should not receive equal prize money. They didn't earn equal money. King had recently become the first woman athlete in any sport to earn more than a hundred thousand dollars in a single season. Rod Laver made $292,000 on the men's tour the same year. That sort of money was brand new in tennis. In 1970, the year Margaret Court captured the Grand Slam, she had earned a bonus of fifteen thousand dollars. Fourteen years later, Martina's bonus would be a million dollars.

Riggs had arrived for the Battle of the Sexes with an armful of red roses. There was a note too. It said, 'For one of the all-time greats in tennis who is just as great a mother.' Court was the most famous mother in tennis. The match, played in California, was held on 13 May 1973, Mother's Day in America. Court had a big serve, good ground strokes, a fine overhead game, and she was an aggressive volleyer. But she had been known to clutch when the pressure was on. Virginia Wade calls her 'the nervous champion'. Court, a hefty woman, with nice big shoulders, may have been particularly nervous about competing against men. In fifty-seven minutes it was over. Court had clutched and lost, 6–2, 6–1.

To avenge the Mother's Day Massacre, the five-foot four-and-a-half-inch-tall Billie Jean King, who had been beaten by Court in two dramatic Wimbledon finals, decided to face Riggs. King, twenty-nine, was the Wimbledon, the US, and the French singles champion, and the leading exponent of equality.

The match would be played after Wimbledon and the US Open in late September.

At Wimbledon, Martina knelt down to touch the grass. This was a holy place for tennis players. In the locker room, though, she couldn't spot anyone great or famous. 'They were all upstairs in the other locker room.' As it was her first time, Martina had been assigned to the windowless basement locker room, the one reserved for peons. 'I didn't find out till the next year when I couldn't find my name on the list and they told me I was upstairs in the better locker room. Someone took me up, and there everybody was.

'I guess you could say my whole career's been defined by Wimbledon,' says Martina. 'I have so many memories. Shoot, I still remember my first match there in seventy-three. I played in a dress I got from Fred Perry, and it was too small.' The match was against the sturdy English rose Christine Truman.

When Truman, the 1961 Wimbledon finalist, looked at the draw she didn't know what to think, so she asked Virginia Wade. 'I said I'd been drawn against the girl with the unpronounceable name, and Virginia Wade warned me, "You want to watch her. She's really good."' On Court 1, chubby, sixteen-year-old, middle-sized Martina beat Truman, six feet tall and sixteen years older, 6–1, 6–4 in the first round despite the fact that her tennis dress kept catching on her bra.

Martina lost in the third round to the freckled, 23-year-old American Patti Hogan who at the time had a certain eminence. Martina's had been an excellent debut, and she enjoyed it. 'There was no pressure on me. I was just happy to be out there playing and getting to know all the players and travelling the world and making my mark.' What are your ambitions, the journalists soon were asking. 'I have plenty, but just say to win Wimbledon.'

In the mixed doubles Martina had the honour of partnering the best Czech tennis player never to have left. This was the year that Jan Kodes would win the Wimbledon men's singles. At Sparta, Kodes had taken her seriously before anyone else had. Kodes says all he did was encourage her 'to keep going to the net'. Now, at Wimbledon, he was equally prepared to trust her. On Court 2 they faced Billie Jean King and Owen Davidson. Trying to impress her heroine whom she had finally met, Martina played terribly. She and Kodes lost. Eventually their opponents won the title.

In the midst of Martina's spiritual communion with the Wimbledon turf, the 1973 championships were being visited by an unheavenly whirlwind of politics. The unrest that had led to the Bedroom Caucus in Houston in 1970 was continuing. Now there were meetings going on in hotel rooms late into the night. At the Gloucester Hotel where many of the players were staying, Billie Jean King instructed the big Dutch player Betty Stove to block the door so none of the sixty-three women in the room could leave before the vote on whether or not a women's players' association would be formed. The vote carried and the Women's Tennis Association was formed during that Wimbledon with the defending champion Billie Jean King as president. Open tennis for men was also going through birth pains, and that year most men boycotted the championships.

Billie Jean King, whose nickname was the Old Lady, had been politicking and playing her way through Wimbledon. When the singles final was delayed by rain, she cracked jokes in the locker room. Postponed, the final was played the next day and the Old Lady, who cursed and berated herself on court as usual, defeated Chris Evert to win the singles title. People spoke of Wimbledon as the Old Lady's house.

Shortly after, came the Bobbie Riggs match which would be

so important to the future of women's tennis. This time Riggs brought his opponent the phallic-shaped candy called Sugardaddy. King's gift to Riggs was a piglet, a living symbol of his male chauvinism. Play began and Billie Jean King pulverized him. For reasons which can be analyzed, but which are at their core irrational, this defeat of the ageing Bobbie Riggs by a woman player in her prime convinced the media and many in its audience that women's tennis was worth paying for. Meanwhile, Martina was beginning to demonstrate that on court.

A month earlier in Toronto, Rod Laver had been in the stands when Martina played the up and coming Australian Wendy Turnbull. Martina won the first set to love. In tennis slang, a love set is called a 'bagel' because a bagel is shaped like a zero. Having bageled her opponent, Martina then very nearly lost the next set and the 6–0, 7–5 match, a sign that the killer instinct a champion needed was not yet properly in place. Laver was impressed anyway. He had noticed Martina's almost unbelievable quickness and deft placements. Martina heard he was telling people that she was a player to watch.

'I lived off that compliment during the fall,' she says. She had trusted her stepfather's judgement. Now she took strength from Laver's. 'If Rod Laver thought I was going to be good, I figured I'd better be.' There was no time for his compliment to go to her head. At the US Open in September she lost in the first round. None the less, her 1973 debut season had been a success. Martina made it to the quarter-finals of the French and the third round at Wimbledon. Not bad.

The next year, at the 1974 Italian Open, she attracted international attention by reaching the final where she lost to Chris Evert but got excellent notices. The British and European tennis correspondents recognized immediately that this was a great and exciting talent even if she wasn't winning yet. She lost in the first round at Wimbledon, where Chris won the title. None the less, Martina had more talent than Chris, whose greatest gifts were her sound but limited number of groundstrokes and above all her coolly focused ability to concentrate. As an athlete, Martina was a natural. Her debut caused a stir in Europe where she was native and where at least until she started swearing at the linesmen, the crowds preferred her to the so very typically American Chris. The teenaged Martina seems to have been blithely unaware of the impact she was making. 'I remember eating a lot of ice cream, blowing up, and putting on about ten pounds,' she says. That year, Martina beat the Dutch player Betty Stove to get to the third round of the US Open where she lost to Julie Heldman, an American.

In 1975, her third year on the international circuit Martina knocked out Margaret Court on her home turf in the quarter-final of the Australian Open, 6–4, 6–3. This win which many have cited as a sign of Martina's growing power should be seen in perspective. Court who had either won or been a finalist at the Open a dozen times was injured and approaching the end of her career. None the less, to be a giant-killer was sweet. Martina made it all the way to what would be her first grand slam final where she lost 6–3, 6–2 to the newer Australian star Evonne Goolagong.

Up to now, Martina had been winning on instinct and innate ability and luck, but with Goolagong she soon realized her strategy lacked something in sophistication. 'Because my back-hand was so lousy I figured everybody else's was too. So that was my strategy, hit it to their backhand and come in. Of course I did that against Evonne too'. Unfortunately, her backhand was nuclear in power.

That year Martina also made the finals at the French Open, where she lost to Chris Evert, but Martina beat Chris twice, in Washington and Chicago. They had played in fifteen matches.

Chris, who wanted to stem the Martina tide, had an unexpected ally. 'Abetted by McDonald's, Chrissie kindly introduced chocolate-chip cookies, burgers and buns to the teenaged Navratilova, who embraced them with an all-consuming vengeance,' says the British sportswriter Sue Mott. Billie Jean King and

Rosie Casals were McDonald's addicts too. The pasta and white meat principle, which would itself be superseded by the dogma of strict vegetarianism, had not yet been widely adopted in sport.

Tennis was going well for Martina, but there was the weight problem, a fashion problem, and she was having difficulties with the Czech Tennis Federation who complained she was becoming 'too Americanized'.

Martina had switched to Teddy Tinling dresses. Tinling, the Hardy Amies of tennis, designed dresses for her that were, shall we say, unusual. The aggressively floral one she would wear at the US Open was a favourite, 'because it's like my personality. Wild.'

Too wild for the Czech bureaucrats to tame. She had stayed in America longer than they had intended her to, competing when and where she saw fit. This was possible to do because she was now earning dollars in the thousands. Another thing the Czech Federation objected to was that she hung out with Chris Evert and Evert's sister and with other top players, instead of Czechs. Billie Jean King, the pre-eminent serve and volleyer, was giving her inheritor Martina pointers. 'I helped Martina. I helped Chris too.' The baseliner Chris would in fact extend the strokes of her game. To the Czechs, though, Martina seemed to be on a perpetual buying spree, her tastes utterly straightforward: only the best. To counter some of the bad influences, the Federation wanted her to play more matches in Europe. Martina preferred the balmy weather of Florida and the well-lit, indoor American circuit where instead of black skies, it rained green dollars.

She ignored the Federation and seemed not to care about the impression her flamboyant tennis dresses were making. There was one time on the West Coast when someone in the crowd tittered as she came out on court. Then someone else. Soon there was a wave of tittering. 'People in the stands giggled because she looked dorky,' remembers the American sports writer Candice Hogan. 'But as soon as she started to play, the crowd stopped giggling.' Those in the stands who knew about tennis recognized at once that here was an extraordinary player. She had it all, the strokes, athleticism, the speed. 'You could tell,' says Hogan. 'You could really tell.'

The BBC's Dan Maskell and *The Times* tennis correspondent Rex Bellamy had noticed too. At Torquay, where she first played in England, both realized she was someone who might someday be a champion – if her nervous temperament didn't let her down.

'If a bad call came or I missed an easy shot, I would just brood about it,' recalls Martina, 'and I'd lose the match because of that. I've always been a perfectionist.'

'She had a little temper problem,' was how the Hall of Fame golfer Sandra Haynie, the woman who would solve it, put it. If Martina got a bad call – linesmen were not professionals – she sometimes got so angry she would lose the next few points. There was some speculation as to whether or not she would get to the top in spite of herself.

At Wimbledon, where she reached the quarter-finals in 1975, the intrepid *Times* man had been intrigued by the very executive-looking briefcase Martina was carrying. Pure yuppie, except yuppie wasn't a term we were using yet. Bellamy was the man who would write approvingly that 'Chris Evert would rather be known as a girl than a tennis player'. Now he was intrigued by a briefcase for a girl tennis player. What did she keep in it? Spare balls or a calculator to add up her prize money? Obligingly, Martina opened it up for him to see. It wasn't a briefcase. In fact it was a portable backgammon set.

As Martina prepared to face Chris Evert at the 1975 US Open semi-final, one of the biggest moments of her career to date, she had trouble keeping her mind on it. The match, which was being played in Forest Hills, New York, would be Chris's fourth bid for the final, but it was only Martina's first. Yet Martina's thoughts kept spiralling to the moment after the match, when she had an important date. Once the match started, though, she was very much there.

In the first set, with Chris down 15–40 on the point that would have deadlocked the set at 4–all, there was a dispute as to whether the ball was actually in or out. The disputed point was replayed, but Martina lost her concentration, and Chris escaped from the 15–40 deficit, winning the set 6–4. Then it happened again in the second set with Chris serving at 3–4, 30–15. In response to Martina's attack, she hit a forehand lob which the lineswoman called in.

Martina thought the ball was two inches out. The lineswoman Pat Brummer said, 'The ball was good. It hit the edge of the line.'

Martina insisted. Brummer, a teaching pro from Newport, Rhode Island, walked to the spot and pointed to the mark.

'She showed me a mark that was five inches away,' Martina said angrily. 'The calls were perfect except for the last one. That really screwed me up.'

Unable to get her mind off it, she lost the remaining nine points of the match. Broken to love in the game that followed the disputed point, Martina slammed her racket to the ground and sarcastically signalled OK to the lineswoman, with a circled thumb and forefinger. She lost what was now their fourteenth match in straight sets, 6–4, 6–4.

'She could have won it if she forgot about that point,' Chris Evert said. 'I think she lost the match on that point. The last three games she was thinking about that one point.'

This was the temperament problem others had noticed. The *New York Times* commented: 'While Martina's husky frame and high-velocity strokes are all woman, her mental commitment often yields to youth. She let her concentration slip.'

'I was very angry. I wore my emotions on my sleeve, but I wasn't able to control it,' says Martina. 'I took it out on the linespeople, but I always took it out on me too.'

Martina may, though, have been right about the call. Chris

Evert said later that she would have accepted a let and replayed the point.

At the net Martina congratulated Chris who put a hand on her shoulder. Chrissie was one of the few people who knew about and approved of Martina's private date.

On the West Coast of America that day, Friday, 5 September 1975, a young woman pointed a loaded gun at President Gerald Ford at close range and was preparing to fire when a secret serviceman wrestled her to the ground. On the east coast, the Governor of New York warned a hostile legislature that only emergency funds would keep police on the mean, crime-infested streets of New York City. And nationwide inflation was up. The day was not an advertisement for America.

That night Martina, who did not put much stock in what she read in the papers because in her country the papers usually printed official lies, walked nervously into the down-at-the-heel offices of the Immigration and Naturalization Service in downtown Manhattan, one of the older parts of the city. When she sat at the desk opposite the American official, eighteen-year-old Martina Navratilova was at last keeping the date which had been ordained soon after she first heard the family story of the theft of her heritage by the Communists.

The American leaned forward and assured Martina Navratilova and her adviser that she would be granted a temporary resident permit which amounted to political asylum. As she was from a communist country, processing her application would be 'very routine'. But at 10.30 p.m. when she walked out of the government building, Martina was jumpy. At night, this was one of the scarier parts of Manhattan, deserted by all but rats and criminals. Martina, half expecting Communists to leap from the darkness, feared they would chloroform her and drag her on to a tanker waiting at the nearby docks. No hooded Eastern Europeans sprang from the shadows. No ordinary mugger hit her on the head. She had successfully tempted fate. Mayhem would come in the morning, when the *Washington Post* broke the story – very quickly for an event that had transpired so late at night. Martina has always said she thought someone in authority had leaked it, perhaps for money, or to a friend. It is equally possible someone in her camp did it, or that the American officials gave out the story as a protection. Once it was public, her defection had to be accepted by the Czech government unless they wanted a major international incident.

The danger now was of being mobbed by the media. It was decided to call a press conference to feed the piranhas of journalism.

'I wanted my freedom,' Martina announced. She was dressed American in jeans and a blue shirt. The loafers on her feet, though, were Gucci. So was the shoulder bag. Her watch and the stacks of bracelets were gold.

Had she chosen America for America or its tennis opportunities?

'Both,' she said thoughtfully, adding, 'Anybody who complains about life here should go to Europe and they would understand. Go to a communist country, go to a socialist country. They would understand then. And they complain it's so expensive here. Let them go to France and see. All the demonstrators here, they're crazy.'

In Czechoslovakia, she had been in her last year at school, would she finish at an American high school? 'What for? I will just play the tour, whenever and wherever I want.' Her base for the moment was in the expensive California enclave of Beverly Hills where her American manager and his family lived. But she would be living the life of a well-heeled tennis nomad. 'My father is my coach,' she explained, then added, quickly, 'he was my coach. I don't think my family is in any trouble now. They told me whatever you decide is all right, it's your life.' The family had planned to defect together during Wimbledon but lost their nerve. When she got a second chance a month later, she took it. At her final Wimbledon, nineteen years later, Martina revealed that only her stepfather had been in her confidence when she finally decided to defect. 'I told my father that

I thought I was going to do it. He said I think you should. He didn't tell my mother. She didn't know.'

'It was terrible for us,' says Jana Navratilova, 'but it was good for her.'

At the time of her defection, it was speculated that in addition to prize money she would make between one and two hundred thousand dollars a year in product endorsements, which were a very new thing in tennis, and more from contracts to play the recently invented World Team Tennis. Martina's total official prize money had risen from $6,100 in 1973, her first year on the circuit, to $36,480 the following year. In 1975, it would more than quadruple to $179,243. But Martina was adamant, 'My decision was not based on money at all.'

In answer to the then perennial question, she said, 'I don't have a boyfriend here, that is not the reason.'

Three months before she defected, Martina had her first lesbian affair. 'I knew I had feelings for women, I wanted to be close to them, but I didn't realize it was sexual until it happened. Then in the morning, I said, uh, I guess I'll be like this for the rest of my life. Because I felt at home, I felt very comfortable with a woman. I realized, this is it. And my life was going to be inherently much more difficult, but this was how it was gonna be, and that was it. I never gave it another thought.'

'I didn't know I was gay until I was eighteen years old,' she said in answer to my question at a press conference. 'I never had any problems with it. You guys have problems with it maybe, but I didn't.'

Defecting, Martina had known, would free her. What perhaps she didn't quite realize was that it would lock her into the international celebrity syndrome, the media snare, from which she would be liberated only by failure or retirement from tennis. Her sporting ability would make her a star, but the media would transform her into a megastar, an icon.

'There is a lot more to being a tennis player than tennis,' the former Wimbledon champion Jim Courier opined once. Martina would soon find that out. That first press conference she gave in New York changed her life inexorably. Whether she knew it or not, she had made a pact with the media, who would give her superstardom, but would retain the right to pry into her soul.

The woman who failed to assassinate the president was notorious for a few months. Martina would be famous for decades. 'Politics had nothing to do with my decision,' she said, somewhat contradictorily, when she defected, 'it was strictly a tennis matter,' meaning perhaps that she was choosing professionalism as much as individualism and democracy.

Withstanding extraordinary political and personal pressures, she would play a new inventive attacking tennis and would decisively change the women's game. In the course of what would be the longest and most successful tennis career ever, Martina was to fire many shots for personal freedom, some of them inadvertently.

Initially, however, Martina's departure was a setback in former Wimbledon champion Jan Kodes's battle against the communist authorities. Kodes had been winning in his attempt to get more freedom of movement for Czech tennis players, including himself. Now he faced real trouble. It was Kodes who had convinced the authorities to let Martina go to Wimbledon when they had got wind of the fact that she and her parents might not come back. When they did come back Martina says people looked at them like ghosts. It was Kodes and Vera Sukova who convinced the authorities to let her go to America again in mid-August of 1975 to prepare for the US Open. Now they would pay for their error of judgement.

'I would cause Vera a lot of problems because of my defection while she was still national coach,' Martina realized later. Vera Sukova, who died a few years later, did still greet her when they met, says Martina, but not as warmly as before. 'Things could never be the same after my defection.'

'My parents never talked about it in front of me,' says Vera's daughter Helena Sukova, 'so I had no idea what my mother, what they were going through. I was ten at the time.'

Jan Kodes had had trouble because he had gone to bat for Martina. For a long time, Kodes did not know if he himself would ever play abroad again.

'It was more difficult for my mother because at the time she was the national coach, and she was the one who was blamed,' says Helena Sukova. 'They tried to blame her for it, and for a long time she had trouble.'

Helena can remember her mother giving Martina coaching. 'I remember her practising with my mother at Sparta. Her sister Jana was also playing at the time.' Jana is more Helena's age. Martina, who played the Pilsen tournament every August, stayed at the house of her friend and doubles partner, who was Vera Sukova's niece.

Kodes believed her defection was unnecessary. With a little patience she could have had everything she wanted anyway. Even today, Kodes, who now heads the Czech Federation, thinks it was unnecessary for Martina to defect. 'For the earlier defectors like Drobny, yes. But things were changing.' He believes they would have changed in time for Martina's career to flourish.

Not everyone agrees, including his sister Vlasta. 'Martina's talent was well recognized but under the system there were constraints to fulfilling it. There were at least five top women, and only two could go to a tournament so the competition for the post was tough. You strove to be one of the top two.' In the midst of a so-called egalitarian society, only in sport was there such cut-throat competition. 'It kept the standard of players high,' says Vlasta. 'But you wouldn't always be chosen.'

By defecting Martina could play every tournament, which was what she needed if she was to become the champion she knew she could be. Yes, it was selfish. She had to be. That very 'selfishness' – a sense of self – was a concomitant of her strength of character. People who queue quietly rarely arrive anywhere first.

The Czech players often had a minder with them, but not a Bulgarian-style heavy. It would be the coach or another player. 'You could go out when you wanted to,' recalled Vlasta. 'You were not watched every moment.' On her first trip to the United States in 1973 Martina travelled with another player. Would-be Bulgarian defectors had to fear darts shot from umbrellas, after which, either dead or unconscious, you would be whisked back behind the iron curtain. To Czechs the barriers to defection were now more psychological than physical. There were no longer the careful body searches. You were even allowed to keep 60 per cent of the money; some reports said eighty.

When Jan Kodes, the first Czech player to make serious money, arrived home with several thousand dollars in cash in his pocket he precipitated a crisis. He had been paid in dollars, which he brought home and showed the president of the Czech Tennis Federation.

'What should I do with it?' Kodes asked nervously.

The official looked uneasily at the money. 'I don't know,' he said. 'Hide it. I will find out.'

For three days Kodes kept the money hidden in his house. 'Regulations had to be established.' Then the bureaucracy made up its mind. 'Some of the money went to the government, some I was allowed to keep.' Martina's official prizewinnings so far for the year 1975 were $126,263. She was second on the Money List. Chris Evert, first, had earned $280,927. Gradually, over the years, Czech players had been allowed to keep a larger portion of their prize money. The *New York Times* reported that the Czech Federation took 20 per cent of all Martina's prize money and the American Inland Revenue Service took 30 per cent of all that was earned in America.

Despite the short-term difficulty it caused some of her compatriots, Martina's defection was beneficial to those who would follow. It was the beginning of the end of the CTF's control of its top players. The two later Czech champions Ivan Lendl and Hana Mandlikova would be allowed to do whatever they wanted to. Both lived in style in America, where they owned property. Although they did not defect, they remained Czech in name and passport only.

Martina's team mates knew for sure she had gone only when they read it in the papers but they weren't surprised. 'It was expected. You have to have a special character for that,' says Vlasta. 'She was a special character. She was able to do it. I admired her for her strength.'

The Czech papers said that Martina had run away because she was scared of failing her school examinations. That didn't fool many Czechs. The newspapers usually lied. At best they printed partial truths. Astute newspaper readers developed a very Czech method of following Martina's successes over the next decade. If you knew Wimbledon was on, and there was no report of it, then you knew Martina had won. Or if the younger Czech player Hana Mandlikova had lost to an unnamed opponent, you could guess who.

Defection is hard for Westerners to understand. It seems disloyal, ungrateful. It was, after all, with every opportunity nature and nurture could grant her and every advantage provided by the Czech tennis system that she had become a champion.

It is characteristic of champions, however, that they want. No matter how much they have, they yearn for more: partly to prove to themselves that they are as good as everyone else, partly to prove to the world that they are better. Instead of gratitude for the Czech system that had spawned her career, Martina and her family saw her success as a way of subverting the system, a way of getting their own back.

And so the most promising Czech player of her generation, of any generation, had not hesitated for long when she saw a chance to defect. Martina's childhood had been a grudge match against the Czech government. She won it. Now she had a shot at the American Dream.

~ 4 ~

A Friend in Texas

The cameras zoom in. Hunched forward in the player's chair at the side of the court, Martina is sobbing. The number three seed who wants so much to be an American has just lost in the first round of the 1976 US Open at Forest Hills. Ruthlessly, the cameras send this image of uncontrollable woe into a million American living rooms. Her face buried in a towel, she is still sobbing. Janet Newberry, the American who won, puts a hand on Martina's shoulder.

It was now a year since Martina's defection and at Forest Hills she had defeated herself, and she knew it. It was not just the loss of a tennis match that she was crying for, it was the defeat of all her hopes. 'Well, after I hit bottom at Forest Hills there was only one way to go, and that was up. Everything had happened too fast for me.' During 1976 she had learned what it was like to be disliked or written off by everyone, including perhaps herself. Two months earlier at Wimbledon, where she reached the semi-final – almost the only highlight in a low season – Martina had accused the line judges of cheating. The incident was widely reported. At Wimbledon, Martina had defeated the French star Françoise Durr and the British number one Sue Barker before losing 6–3, 4–6, 6–4 to the iron will and steely double-fisted backhand of Chris Evert. But at the Open, she had fallen to a much less gifted player. It was widely believed that Martina would never achieve what she wanted, what her natural talent could have ordained for her. And when she played Chris Evert, the crowds cheered Chris.

To the American fans watching from the wooden bleachers, and to those curled up with a can of beer in front of what was then often called the 'boob tube', Forest Hills was, with the possible exception of Wimbledon, the main event of the tennis season. In the Forest Hills locker room after a successful Wimbledon, Chris Evert, munching on a chocolate brownie, had said, 'People in England were so formal. Here they come like it was a baseball game.' There was plenty of ice to put into your Pepsi too. Forest Hills was noisy and unmannerly and full of the sort of vigour and energy that made it quintessentially American. If you wanted to be a heroine to Americans you had to win the US Open.

Martina had arrived at what was even to non-Americans the second most important grand slam of the year in a terrible state physically. Twenty-five or so pounds overweight, carrying 167 pounds, she was the embodiment of too much high living and too little training.

It was now close to the end of a tennis year which Chris Evert had dominated, losing only five of her eighty matches. Martina, who had played her three times that year, won once, at the Virginia Slims of Houston, but Chrissie would end the 1976 season as both the Wimbledon and the US Open champion.

Under the guidance of her new coach Sandra Haynie, Martina had, almost despite herself, managed to reach her first Wimbledon semi-final. There, berating herself as well as the linesmen, she had fallen to Chris. Getting to the semi in her physical state, in any state, was a considerable achievement. But it was not the culmination of her dreams, not what she had expected. Unfit, she was miserable, and now even tennis wasn't working.

In the year following her defection, Martina had become a poor little rich girl. She missed her family. 'I call them and talk for as long as an hour and a half each week. But I don't want to go back to Czechoslovakia.' The telephone bills were not a problem. Ever since she had come over – 'come over' was a term preferable to 'defected' – the problem had been loneliness. 'I was eighteen years old, like a kid leaving home to go to college. But all of a sudden I was alone, four or five thousand miles from my family.' She was facing the crises any adolescent faces. 'And I was doing it in front of the whole world. I think I would have been less turbulent had my life been more private, but that was impossible.'

Martina drowned her sorrows in expensive purchases of cars and jewellery and clothes. She owned a pride of gold rings and bracelets and watches. 'I get carried away in jewellery stores,' she quipped. 'People are always asking me if I am in the jewellery business.' At a time when American materialism was under assault by the best minds of her generation, Martina embraced the ugly Americanhood of 'conspicuous consumption' without a qualm. Many who witnessed it used the image of a child in a sweet shop.

'It was all new to her,' recalls Sandra Haynie, who would become the major influence in her life for the next three years. 'Not to fault her, this was a world she had never been exposed to before, all things an awful lot of Americans take for granted, being able to buy a car or being able to buy a watch.'

'Instead of candy she was buying designer clothes and luxury automobiles,' Billie Jean King would write in her history of women's tennis, *We Have Come a Long Way*. 'Martina's immaturity was apparent on the tennis court as well, and she agonized over every failure, no matter how small. One bad line call could snap her concentration and send her to defeat.'

At first, Martina did not see that there was any problem. 'I don't think I thought that I needed any help. I had it all figured out. I was twenty years old,' she says. 'I thought I could just rely on my talent for the game.'

Even though she was the most gifted player to arrive on the scene in decades, this was a great mistake. To succeed in the competitive world of Court, King and Evert, she would have to improve her mind, her body, and her game. The flaws in her temperament were just as damaging to her prospects as the lack of physical conditioning. Her play was good, but she needed more strokes to her game, more finesse, and a less simplistic court strategy. You couldn't just play to your opponent's backhand. Becoming a champion was a tall order. Her greatest ally, at the start of what would be a career-long journey, was Sandra Haynie, who had been a factor in her life for some months. Now Martina would buckle down and really listen to Haynie.

One of the world's best golfers, Sandra Jane Haynie was the first of two native Texans who would change Martina's life. Born and bred in Fort Worth (where later Martina would also live with Judy Nelson), Haynie is still regarded as one of the all-time hundred best golfers, male or female. Certainly she was a giant of the women's game.

Born in 1943, she was thirty when Martina arrived on the world tennis scene and, like Miss Jean Brodie, in her prime. In 1974, her best year professionally, Haynie won six tournaments including the two majors, the Ladies Professional Golf Association Championship and the US Women's Open, which she won by a point with birdies on the last two holes. Haynie knew how to be cool in a crisis. Martina was by her own admission coming apart at the seams. The calm professionalism which Haynie was known for in golf was precisely what was lacking in Martina's tennis.

They met two years after Martina's arrival in the United States, at the women's Superstars, a popular television sports competition. Martina was a participating athlete. Haynie had friends who were. 'I was just there and watching my friends make fools out of themselves. I was introduced to her. Martina had just won a tennis tournament. It was in Houston, I think. She had defected some six months prior to when I met her, her English still wasn't very good.'

The Superstars involves top athletes participating in sports in which they usually are not experts. At the practice session, though, Martina had a small culture shock. She looked at the bowling ball, and said, 'I don't know how to do this.' Bowling, a major leisure pastime in America, was largely unknown in Prague.

Haynie happened to be in hearing distance. 'I said, I'm not an expert either, but I can kinda show you the principle. I kinda helped her through a few of those things.' Rowing a boat, for instance. 'We kinda got talking, and it was just one of those things, where you know she was a little bit lost, having defected from her family, and here she was at the age of twenty and having made much deeper decisions than any of us would ever have to make in a lifetime, much less at a very young age. She was a little overwhelmed, I think.'

Haynie took her under her wing. 'We just kinda got to talking a little bit, I went on to play a golf tournament, she came and watched one day, and then she went off to a tennis tournament.'

Haynie lived in Dallas. Martina was coming to Dallas for the Virginia Slims tournament. 'I said, well you're welcome to stay in the house if you like. She ended up staying for a while.'

It seemed to Haynie that Martina 'was into that syndrome of the fast lane, if you will.' Too much, too soon, of the wrong sort of living. 'She had lost her support system when she left Czechoslovakia,' says Haynie, who would provide an alternative one. 'We just kinda struck up a friendship. We were kind of talking about concentration, motivation, working on this, that and the other. Through a period of time she just kept talking more and more and more to me.

'Then finally I just was kinda starting to burn out on golf a little bit, and she said would you work with me a little bit. I said sure. I knew zippo about tennis basically. I was truly well versed in a lot of sports, but the strategy and stuff like that, it was not my forte. I had never been exposed to a racket sport but there's a lot of common threads and a common bond between athletes and the tools that they have to have to be good.'

Martina told Haynie that she wanted to be the best in the

world. Even then, her goal was absolutely to be number one.

'Well, getting there's the easy part,' Haynie said. 'Staying there's the hard part.'

The moment was opportune for both of them. Haynie was having trouble with her hands as well as feeling somewhat burned out. 'So I kinda quit playing golf for a while, had hand surgery, and we started working together. She didn't have roots, and she needed that for herself. So I encouraged her. She wanted a house and I encouraged her to look here, so she bought a house in Dallas, and we learned how to change our diet from Big Macs to vegetables and chicken and salad. We learned to go work out and to make working out fun.'

Martina and Haynie shared the three-bedroom house. 'I think everything sort of settled down for me from that point,' recalls Martina. 'That's when things started for me.'

The house itself was fairly ordinary by American standards. 'The pool filled the whole backyard,' says Haynie. It was a small pool in a small backyard. 'We moved there together, from about seventy-seven to maybe seventy-nine, a couple of years, and lived there with a poodle I found, called Racket.

'We'd go to the park. I felt it was important. She thought working out might be running all the time. I said no, you need to do sprints because everything you do is start and stop and change direction. So we'd go to the park and we'd throw a football and I'd say cut right, cut left. We also started playing a lot of racketball.'

This togetherness did not extend to weight training.

'No, I got her in a place to do all that but I let her do that by herself. She worked with weights in a private health club. She started shedding weight, she lost about thirty or so pounds just within eight months. We had to go through a thing where her timing was changing and she was getting to the ball quicker. So she kinda went through a period when she wasn't playing as well because she was getting to the ball quick, her racket preparation wasn't there.'

The first year, Martina did a lot of sweating she wasn't used to. She was also always having to play tennis.

One day she said to Haynie, 'I think you're trying to kill me.'

'She thought you practise a little bit and go play,' said Haynie. 'You've gotta get match tough, and the only way to do that is play. That first year, I don't know how much we travelled but it was a ton.'

The idea was that Martina should play and play. That year she played a long season, forty weeks. All those matches didn't leave a lot of time for working out. But she was playing enough tennis and was discarding some bad habits along the way. Martina was coming out of the slump. They had changed her timing, worked on her conditioning, and were now dealing with that little temper problem. And Martina was starting to win some tournaments. The Haynie connection was bearing fruit.

The fact that Haynie didn't know anything about tennis seemed to worry a lot of people. Several people said to Martina, 'Why would you listen to a golfer? She doesn't know anything about tennis.'

'No,' Martina would say, 'but she does know how to win. That's the common ground I have to have right now.'

What Haynie was good at was what Billie Jean King would also be good at, motivating and helping Martina to focus. 'She also had a little bit of a temper problem in the beginning. We worked on how to turn that into positive energy and how to use that in a match to help, as opposed to letting it destroy the next several points, then the whole game, then the whole set, and then possibly the match.'

It was all too clear that the problem had not been fully overcome when Martina's game collapsed in the last set of the 1977 Wimbledon quarter-final, which she lost to Betty Stove 9–8, 3–6, 6–1. Martina won six tournaments that year, five more than in 1976, and reached the semi at the US Open where she lost to the Australian Wendy Turnbull, 2–6, 7–5, 6–4.

In 1978, Billie Jean King, sidelined by injury, added her expertise. Now Martina had two of them reading her the riot act. 'I had a bad foot, so I started helping Sandra, working on Martina's endurance, forcing her to go all out, keeping her pulse up for twenty minutes at a clip. I kept telling her, too, that when things go wrong, don't moan and slump and slink around. Instead use adversity to get your gumption up and fight back.'

Haynie realized that, 'It can mushroom on you real quick. You have to know what pushes your buttons. I always thought that she and McEnroe had a lot in common. They expected so much of themselves they were really unable to accept a mistake.' She told Martina, 'If you get mad, you have to quiet talk yourself and not dwell on it.'

'Yeah, but how?' Martina would say.

'Turn that energy, refocus yourself. They made that call six points ago, well, it's a little late now.'

There were no mantras, though it was the 1970s; no special devices. 'It's just understanding mistakes are gonna happen,' says Haynie. 'Learn by 'em and turn 'em loose.'

Instead, Martina was dwelling on the errors – hers or the linesman's, it didn't matter, it was unproductive, they were dragging her down. She never lacked confidence but she was going through such transition, playing at thirty pounds less.

'The first year or so the WTA would allow me to sit close to court,' Haynie continues. 'It seemed to keep Martina calm and if she wanted to jabber at somebody she could jabber at me instead of at the umpires. From time to time she thought she hit a line and they called it out, she might look over at me. I nodded my head, yeah, the ball was out. Sometimes it wasn't. And she learned to turn loose of it. It didn't continue to eat on her.'

Other times Martina would blame herself. 'Oh, I can't believe I'm playing this bad,' she would say.

'You're not playing that bad,' Haynie would call out. 'Keep on.'

'At that time they didn't have a rule against it, but I really wasn't coaching because I didn't know that much about tennis. It wasn't like I could say, you're taking the racket too far back

74

on the serve, or you're too upright. It wasn't anything instructional. It was just, That's all right, you're playing the game, let's go. Move on. It was just encouragement.'

Haynie, now a member of the nomad tennis tribe, had the run of the tour including the Wimbledon locker room. Her 'coaching' from the sidelines was encouraged because it tamed the wild one.

∼ 5 ∼

The First Time

Now Martina was on the road back. The start of the new year 1978 was marked by her third straight triumph over the blonde-haired, fifteen-year-old tennis prodigy, Tracy Austin, who was five foot two but still growing. 'Can you imagine the headlines if I lost, beaten by a fifteen-year-old?' Martina asked at the Los Angeles Virginia Slims tournament after her straight sets, quarter-final victory. All the pressure had been on 21-year-old Martina, and none on the adolescent Tracy. 'Tracy makes us all feel like old ladies.' A quotable exaggeration, but the pressure was real and it would continue.

In March, at the Dallas Virginia Slims, Martina who was on a thirty-seven-match winning streak, again faced Tracy, who had never beaten her. Again it was in the quarter-finals. It was a Friday night, and Moody Coliseum had a record crowd. Already the hype was young versus old. Tracy, with high hopes but little expectation of success, won the first set, 6–3. Enough of tempting fate. Martina, the top seed, got down to business and won the second, 6–2. At 5–2 in the third set, Martina was serving for the match when Tracy hit a gorgeous passing shot, then another, then a crafty cross-court backhand. Martina was broken, but the score was still 5–3. Many who were there say Martina 'choked'. Of course, young Tracy also seemed to be inspired. She won three of the next four games to arrive at

6–6. The crowd of nine thousand cheered so fervently, Martina pressed her hands to her ears. It was her home crowd. Now the match would go to a tie-break; whoever reached five points first would be the winner. At 4–2 in the tie-break, Tracy was leading because Martina misjudged a couple of shots which went into the net, unforced errors. At 5–4, she won the tie-break and the match. She jumped up and down excitedly. The crowd was ecstatic. Martina, with tears in her eyes, congratulated Tracy warmly and tousled her hair.

Tracy would never forget. 'Martina Navratilova has always been one of the people I admire in tennis,' she would say years later. She would also always count her as a good friend. 'People are surprised when I say that, figuring that Chris would have been a better friend than Martina was, but that wasn't so. How nice that was of her,' Tracy would say after some gesture by Martina, 'but that's just the way she is.' Many players would find that Martina was generous and good, a real 'sweetheart', but the crowd and the linesmen thought otherwise.

That July, in the seeded players' locker room, which had windows overlooking the far courts and floral-print sofas, Martina was trying to prepare herself for her first Wimbledon final, which would be against Chris. The moment was not as she and her stepfather might have dreamed. There had been an unpleasantness in the third set of the semi-final, an argument with the umpire because of Evonne Goolagong's scream when she pulled a calf muscle as she hit a shot. The ball was good, and Martina probably could have returned it, but had stopped playing to see what was the matter. 'I stopped out of concern for her.' Martina was the server, and it was break point. The umpire refused to replay the point. 'The crowd was upset that I wanted to play a let, and I was going crazy because I could have played the ball.' However, Martina broke back and won 2–6, 6–4, 6–4. To many in the crowd, she had seemed more concerned about the point than about her injured opponent. 'It was funny,' Martina mused, 'because here I got to my first Wimbledon final and I'm the bad guy.'

Soon it would be time to depart for Centre Court, to walk under the much-quoted lines inscribed over the doorway through which all players – even the bad guys – must walk on their way to Centre Court:

> If you can meet with Triumph and Disaster
> And treat those two impostors just the same

And if you can treat them the same, then what? Well, as the crucial line of Rudyard Kipling's poem says, 'Then, you are a man, my son.' This is not usually mentioned.

Meanwhile, on the other side of London there was a very different scenario. The impoverished tennis fan who some years later would write the *Wimbledon Quiz Book* had never been in a betting shop before. The place was full of men and cigarette smoke. The one behind the counter said to her, 'What horse do you want, love?'

'I don't want to bet on a horse.'

'What dog, then?'

'No, it's a person. I want to bet on Martina Navratilova to win Wimbledon.'

'Bet on Chris Evert, love,' he said. 'She'll win.' The world number one had already won Wimbledon twice, and Navratilova wasn't a name the bookmaker knew.

Anne McArthur put five pounds on Martina anyway. The odds were five to one. But later as she watched the match on television, Anne McArthur's blood and mug of tea began to go cold.

Martina on the court of dreams had her worries too. Chris Evert seemed to be in overdrive. No matter how deft, how unexpected Martina's shot, Chris returned it. And those passing shots hurt, one of them literally, when it grazed Martina's temple. Chris took the first set, an utter hash, 6–2.

Haynie, in the players' guest box, was looking bleak, but not

John Lloyd. The so-called Adonis of British tennis, sitting with some friends in the players' enclosure, had had his second date with Chris the night before the final.

Martina glanced ruefully at the wooden racket that was letting her down. It had defeated Tracy Austin in the round of sixteen and, eventually, Evonne. Now, though, on the backhand it seemed to belong to the enemy. Each time Chris played to it, traitorously, it gave Chris the point. Chris was the one wresting the keys of the Ferrari from the poison snakes and stepping on the accelerator. Martina was stuck in traffic in a second-hand Ford. In the semi-final, it had taken the loss of the first set to get her into gear. She had had to tempt fate before the adrenaline would flow. Now, once again at crisis point, Martina at last turned the key in the ignition of her mental Ferrari. The match immediately became a battle royale. Chris wasn't giving anything away. *She* was a winner. One of the first games of the set went to deuce five times, but Martina took the game. It was the turning point of the match. Great champions win on the great occasions. Something in her system kicked into gear. It was clear now to everyone that she *wanted* to win. And the set was hers, 6–4.

But Chris wanted to win too, and Chris knew how to win. Did Martina? She was leading 2–0 in the third set, exhilarated, when Chris, who looked tired, got a second wind, and hit back, breaking her serve at love to take a 4–2 lead.

There is a view that an excellent baseliner will always prevail over an equally excellent serve-and-volley player. Inexorability winning over panache. There was only one way she could win now. By breaking the speed limit. Daring to take risks that few players would chance in a Wimbledon final, Martina broke Chris's serve and held her own to level at 4–4. On a winning point, she kissed her wooden racket. But Chris rallied and teetered on the brink of victory at 5–4. Martina did not crack; Chris did. 'I just served really well,' recalls Martina. 'I got all my first serves in.' She won twelve of the next thirteen points, winning the set and the 1½-hour match, 2–6, 6–4, 7–5. She raised her arms high in triumph. She was the Wimbledon champion. At last. She had finally shown the killer instinct. At the net, to which both players rushed, the one to congratulate, the other to be congratulated, Chris tousled Martina's hair affectionately. The crowd was cheering. Haynie was beaming. The photographers' lenses were zooming in on Martina. It was wonderful to win. Unforgettable ecstasy. No longer a bad guy, she was a glorious champion. She wept. 'I remember how I felt when I won for the first time,' she said at her final Wimbledon. 'It was such a pure feeling.'

Inside the Wimbledon locker room, Haynie congratulated her warmly. Later, they were going out to celebrate. Martina left to go to the press. Chris was still in the locker room. Chris was upset. As joyful as Haynie felt for Martina, she felt sad for Chris. 'Chris was a friend and I didn't know what to say. They'd played a great match, they'd both left a lot on the court, I tried to stay out of the way.'

Chris came over and said, 'Do you mind if I sit here?'

'No, not at all.'

'She just kinda was sitting there,' Haynie recalls. After a few minutes Haynie said, 'You OK?'

Chris answered, 'I will be.'

Haynie sat there with her for a time.

Four days later, the WTA computer anointed Martina world number one. To her friends, Chris put the defeat down to the distraction of love. Years later, when Martina was retiring, Chris said, 'That was one year in 1978 that I should have won, and I lost to Martina because I was in love.'

Yet, still in love two months later, Chris defeated Pam Shriver to win the US Open. Six-foot-tall, sixteen-year-old Pam was just five months older than Tracy Austin with whom she was developing a rivalry similar to Chris and Martina's. It would never attain the same grandeur, but the tensions would be equal. Tracy had watched in the stands as Pam presented Martina with yet another defeat in a US Open semi-final. Twice interrupted by rain, Martina and Pam's semi was none the less tense all the way to the second-set tie-breaker in which Martina saved three match points with winners before going down 7–6, 7–6. It was her third US Open semi-final. Except for that terrible 1976 first-round defeat to Janet Newberry – that nadir of her career – Martina had made every US Open semi-final since the match she played on the day she defected.

The young Tracy Austin looked like Chris and played like Chris. She herself says, 'I was in the Chris Evert mould.' Imagine having two of them to contend with. In January, 1979, Tracy Austin beat Martina in Washington. But Martina pulled her game together and triumphed over Tracy in their next six matches. During one of them – in Los Angeles in February – the young Austin had an indication that she had possibly had too much hard play too soon. 'It was the first time I really had trouble with my back.' Injuries would put her out of the game when she was twenty-one, and although she would make a comeback years later, she would never again attain a high world ranking. At Wimbledon that year, Martina also beat her in the semis, 7–5, 6–1.

On 17 April 1979, Martina was one of a hundred or so guests at Chris Evert's wedding in Fort Lauderdale. Rosie Casals was there too. Ana Leaird, the WTA publicity director who was Chris's best friend, was a bridesmaid. By the time she married, at the age of twenty-four, Chris Evert had already won the US Open four times and Wimbledon twice. She took John Lloyd's name.

Particularly at a time when the women's movement was riding so high, this was a conservative choice. Her relaxed, open-minded attitude towards lesbians on the circuit was therefore in a sense surprising. Some of Chris Evert's best friends were lesbians. All of them including Martina were in the closet with the press and the public, but of course Chris knew. 'I never felt threatened by the fact that some of the girls who I really liked – and who were good friends – were; it didn't bother me at all. I am not, but I never judged them on it.'

Chris had been world number one for four years. Despite the fact that the balance of power in their tennis relationship appeared to be changing, Martina and Chris were still friends.

They were, though, very different characters. Chris could fool around with you, go shopping with you, be a great friend, and then turn ruthless on court. Martina needed to get better at that.

Just before a match Chris wasn't your friend any more; she wasn't friendly to anyone. She would psych herself up with a display of temper and tantrums. 'Before a match she could be a bitch,' Ana Leaird says in Chris and John Lloyd's joint autobiography. Then she would usually win. 'Sometimes I could tell she was going to lose simply because she was being too nice.'

Martina showed her nerves by more or less falling apart. 'She usually goes through a spell where at ten minutes before a match she goes into a total panic,' says Billie Jean King. 'And she goes, "hghhhhhh"' – Billie mimes wide-eyed, screechy terror. 'Then she's OK if we talk for like two or three minutes. About anything.' Nerves would beset Martina until her retirement.

It had been rumoured that the Duchess of Kent would use her influence to ensure that Martina's mother could be present at the 1979 Wimbledon. Martina had mentioned to the duchess at the previous Wimbledon how much she missed her parents. The British government may or may not have put pressure on the Czechs – they certainly didn't admit to it – but this time a *vystupni viza* was granted. Jana Navratilova's exit visa arrived none too soon, but she was there for the 1979 Wimbledon final when Martina again faced Chris who was playing for the first time as Mrs Lloyd.

It is always difficult for a defending champion to step on to Centre Court. There is a certain cockiness, a knowledge that you have been there, faced the best, and prevailed. But there are also nerves, misgivings, a reputation to defend. And you lack the simple yearning you once had to be Wimbledon champion for you are champion already. None the less, Martina did it. As she won the last point for a 6–4, 6–4 victory, Jana Navratilova, ecstatic, jumped to her feet, hands high above her head, clapping, clapping, clapping.

At the same Wimbledon, Martina partnered Billie to her twentieth Wimbledon title, a new all-time Wimbledon record. Since 1975, Billie had been tied for the record of nineteen with Elizabeth Ryan. It is hard to overestimate how important such records are to the people who hold them. On the day before that match in which Billie seemed likely to break her record, Elizabeth Ryan, eighty-seven, collapsed at Wimbledon and died on the way to the hospital.

Martina soon ended the doubles partnership, and Billie was furious. 'When she decided to junk me as her doubles partner in 1980 so she could team up with Pam Shriver,' Billie wrote in her autobiography, 'Martina just went ahead and did it. I mean, she never said a word to me; the woman is the last to know, right?'

Months went by, Billie says, and even screaming at Martina didn't elicit an explanation. Billie retaliated in print. 'I've often doubted that Martina cared that much for tennis. Instead, I think she primarily loves what tennis will bring her. It doesn't matter what it is, so long as it is an acquisition.' The rift in their friendship would heal, but Billie would never quite forget the pain of being dropped. Nor would her next doubles partner Pam Shriver, who was also dropped.

Early in 1979 Martina's grandmother Babicka had come to visit Martina and Haynie in Texas. Babicka found America strange but wonderful. Seeing the house through her grandmother's eyes made Martina aware again of how far she had come. An average middle-class American house, it had seemed to Martina, with 3500 square feet, carpeting, and three TVs with remote control. No one had remote control in Czechoslovakia, and when Martina was living there, Grandma didn't even have a TV set. Grandma was so impressed that she would walk around the house on the soft carpeting and say, 'And you did this all by yourself.'

At the tennis tournament Martina was playing in Dallas, what impressed Babicka most was Chris Evert. 'You're *the* Chris Evert?' Babicka asked in Czech. Chris gave her a kiss and a warm embrace whenever they met at that tournament or in Madison Square Garden in New York where Martina and Haynie and Babicka went for the Avon championships. Babicka was delighted when Martina beat Tracy Austin in the finals.

In New York, when they ate at the Czech Pavilion restaurant, Babicka was introduced to the manager, a Czech who had once been the world figure-skating champion. Babicka was excited to meet a Czech household name.

Babicka was the first member of the family to visit. None of the others had been able to get the necessary Czech exit visas. As Babicka was old and not likely to defect – or if she did it would be one less burden on the state – she was given an exit permit, says Martina. Babicka was then eighty-three or eighty-four; Martina is not sure which. The three of them, Martina, Babicka and Haynie, got on fine. Haynie had a bright pink tracksuit which she wore around the house. On her last day, Babicka told Martina how much she liked it. 'When I told Haynie, she went into her room and took it off and gave it to my grandmother to take home to Czechoslovakia.' Babicka left her dressing gown for Martina. Martina kept it and would sometimes press her face against it, feeling close to Babicka.

Some time after Babicka's visit, Martina and Haynie began to drift apart emotionally and mentally. In her autobiography, Martina implies that life with her friend, coach and manager Haynie, who didn't go out a lot, became a little boring. 'Haynie was happy sitting around watching TV.'

'The age difference, I think, had a lot to do with it,' admits Haynie, who had done all her partying. With Haynie, though, getting a lot of rest wasn't just the easy option, it was a professional principle. 'On the tour, getting rest and having a lot of down time, that was important to me.' When they parted, Haynie was roughly the age Martina is now.

Younger Martina wanted something different. She was still evolving, and had much to discover in life. 'I was trying to find the world outside.' Haynie was philosophical: 'I felt I had done all I could do for her, she'd started being a consistent winner and performer. I had healed my body and my mind and I was kinda ready to go back and start playing golf. It was time for her to move on. It was time for me to move on too.'

This was also true of the financial side of Martina's life. Money was as ever an important factor. Long ago, she had asked Sandra Haynie to oversee all her business. 'I started handling everything. I'm glad I did because she felt very safe and very protected, but at the same time she got to a point where she needed to step on.'

Martina decided to become a client of Mark McCormack's giant IMG, which is the world's most powerful sports agency. Chris Evert is also a client. They were to get endorsement contracts, book exhibition matches, and otherwise look after their new client Martina with their vast legal and financial expertise, and would take a percentage of her earnings. In everything they do, IMG is expert in extracting the grandest fee possible. Martina has complained about having too few endorsements. It may be that this conservative, Midwest-based agency, even if they were known as the best, were not the best agents to market Martina who was not a conservative 'product'. Rita Mae Brown, the novelist who would soon be important in Martina's life, would later satirize sports agents – and everybody else in the tennis scene – in her novel *Sudden Death*.

Eighteen years after the cameras zoomed in on her despair at the US Open, as a comment on the Jennifer Capriati drugs scandal, Martina would say, 'Let's hope this is rock bottom for her. As the song says, when you hit rock bottom there are two ways to go, sideways and straight up. So we will hope she will go straight up, realize she was self-destructing, and get her life-act together again.' Martina had experienced her adolescent growing pains in public at exactly the same age. Eighteen-year-old Jennifer Capriati was found by police in a Florida motel room in which there were illegal drugs. Although the young man with her insisted that Jennifer had had no drugs, just a little alcohol and a little sex, Capriati entered a private drug rehab clinic. Martina had never been charged with possession of illegal substances, but she knew about hitting rock bottom. In her own view, at the US Open in 1976, and in the months leading up to it and following it, she had hit what she regarded as rock bottom. From that abyss, two years later, she had climbed to victory on Wimbledon Centre Court. Now she was her own woman. In every respect, it was time to move on.

━ 6 ━

An Affair to Remember

The young Englishman peering out of the bathroom window at the view saw his hostesses, Martina and Rita Mae, strolling arm in arm through the grounds of their Virginia country estate. With their two Japanese dogs yapping at their feet, the women seemed tremendously at ease with each other. Martina in the perennial jeans jacket was the taller, but Rita Mae Brown, who was nearly eleven years older, was socially the more dominant. It was Rita Mae, the novelist, whose tastes and friends filled the twenty-room house. Martina was the quiet one, her tennis trophies tucked away in the gym. Martina was so quiet that at first he had wondered if her English was deficient. It wasn't.

That silly, mildly off-colour joke she had made the night they had the joke-telling contest had shown that her English was nicely nuanced. He couldn't really say what it was that caused Martina to seem somewhat withdrawn on the big social occasions at Flordon, as the house was called. Today, though, Martina and the eloquent, ever elegant, dark-haired Rita Mae both seemed more than content. As he watched, the two women embraced, and half as a parody of the movies, half for real, legs entwined, kissing, toppled over into the long grass. Suddenly, it was all for real. Adam Mars-Jones realized he was not embarrassed to have seen them in such a romantic moment. They seemed happy, they probably wouldn't have minded. He also thought he shouldn't look any longer.

It was August 1980. Martina and Rita Mae had started their relationship slowly, months after their first date. Now, their relationship was in full flower.

That first meeting had been lunch at the Tobacco Company restaurant in Richmond, Virginia, in August of 1978. Only a month before, Martina had won Wimbledon for the first time. There was a third party at the lunch, the mutual friend, a tennis player, who had arranged the meeting. In January, Martina made the next move. 'Out of the blue she just called me up and we just started talking. I thought she was a lot of fun. She was on the road, I had a farm to run, so I really didn't see her for six to eight weeks after she started calling. Then I finally met her at a tournament in Chicago, and that was really nice. I finally got to spend some time with her.'

Despite the distraction, Martina defeated Tracy Austin in the final 6–3, 6–4. Perhaps partly because Martina associated Chicago with love, it was to become one of her favourite tournaments, and partly because Martina associated their love with tennis success, her affair with Rita Mae Brown blossomed into a relationship.

The author of the hilariously comic *Rubyfruit Jungle* and *Six of One* was famous not only as a novelist, but as a lesbian novelist. If the tennis player who was world number one wanted to be discreet about her private life, Rita Mae was not the woman to date.

'I didn't think about my image,' says Martina. 'I didn't say I'm not gonna fall in love with you because you're a well-known lesbian writer.' In life as in tennis Martina would always take risks and play at lightning speed and from the net. She suggested they move in together.

Rita Mae wasn't sure. 'I can't say I wasn't eager, it's just when somebody's twenty-one, they think love is fabulous and it'll solve all their problems, and you just kinda jump in with both feet. That's part of the wonder of being young. I was thirty-two. I was just a little more slow.'

Martina had also fallen in love with the rolling hills of the Virginia countryside, which, she says, 'reminded me of my part of Czechoslovakia'. Now they jointly owned a house with an oak library and nine acres. There were statues on the patio, formal gardens, six bathrooms, a swimming pool and a tennis court that hadn't been used for a long, long time. When they bought the place, it was already called Flordon. When Rita Mae says the word, her southern drawl makes it sound like three syllables. The house, with its acres of verdant grounds, was situated just outside Charlottesville. This meant it was near the University of Virginia and that was important to Rita Mae who yearned to teach there in the English department. To the head of the department, a conservative southern gentleman writer, Rita Mae was an anathema, but she often entertained more junior members of the English department and their husbands or wives. Later, Rita Mae would in fact teach there. Meanwhile, at the parties Martina and Rita Mae hosted, and from Rita Mae's friends who visited, Martina was learning the ways of literary intellectuals.

In Haynie, Martina had chosen a great champion to teach her to be a champion. 'She was like a guru to me for three years,' Martina says. Now, to educate her mind and sensibility, and perhaps to learn more about the ways of love, Martina turned to a 'sophisticated lady'. Rita Mae was a quadruple mixture of prima donna and Southern Good Old Gal, feminist and literary light. Martina was pure tennis champion, a village girl who had developed expensive, almost vulgar tastes. The old guru Haynie had offered the quiet, wholesome, sporting life; Rita Mae, the new mentor, commingled culture and glamour. She would clean up Martina's act without limiting her parameters. That, I believe, is what Martina thought. Thought is perhaps too strong a word. It would have been at the beginning fairly unconscious. It usually is. Rita Mae, for example, liked to dress up. There had been some controversy over the glamorous cover photograph of *Six of One*. She had fought that battle — saying when it was not the thing to say — that what women want to do is fine, and if you want to project a particular image it's up to you; it isn't ideological. This was when most feminists weren't wearing eye make-up on moral grounds.

Over the years, as Martina built her life, she would turn to experts repeatedly. In love and in professional life, Martina would choose one mentor after another. She says Rita Mae Brown liberated her intellect. Unlike some, who are what they are, and stay that way no matter how many honours or riches they acquire, Martina would grow and grow. The young Martina appeared to be earnest and emotional. Rita Mae would help to inform the wry sense of humour. Martina was much more interesting than the static types, and would develop and evolve into a dominant, fascinating, many-faceted woman, who does not like anyone to second-guess her motives. 'Don't tell me what I'm thinking,' she tells the media. 'Don't make assumptions. Ask me.'

Their relationship seemed to be very easy: buddies who had something very sexual going. At the same time, like a royal couple, when they returned from a tennis tournament they had to be welcomed back to the house with a certain amount of ritual.

Flowers would be arranged around the house. Martina and Rita Mae expected the refrigerator to be stocked, so Becky, a graduate student from the university who looked after things, would take one of the cars — there were several just sitting there — and drive to the local gourmet shop Foods of All Nations, which was about halfway between Flordon and town.

There she would more or less shop at random for luxury foods to put into the fridge. The food didn't necessarily correspond to any future use, it might or might not be eaten. It was a showpiece of a fridge, its function less utilitarian than symbolic. When you opened the fridge, you saw not the commodities, but the concept of powerful, influential, rich women at home.

Once, Martina and Rita Mae drove over to the gourmet shop themselves and in the extravagance of the moment, bought a large amount of caviar which, when they opened it at home, turned out to be bad. They, or more likely one of their two employees, Becky and Kathy, asked for a replacement. They had about a spoonful of it when it arrived to make sure it was OK, and then forgot about it. Every now and then, Kathy, shocked by this waste, would secretly skim off a layer of eggs, doing it very carefully so as to leave a perfectly flat surface. But nobody really bothered. Eventually the caviar had to be thrown away.

When they were at Flordon, Martina and Rita Mae would tend to surface about four o'clock in the afternoon, at which time they might run into Adam Mars-Jones, the tall, dark, big-boned Englishman coming back from the university library on his bicycle. He was a graduate student there himself and had been invited to stay at the house by Becky. He was roughly the same age as Martina and entering the same profession as Rita Mae. Rita Mae was delighted when she heard his first book would soon be published. She liked to have a literary coterie. He is now well known for both his film criticism and his fiction.

Becky and Kathy, also a graduate student, were under the impression that Rita Mae was their employer. However, Martina and Rita Mae funded everything jointly. 'We shared,' Rita Mae says. 'Martina's great about stuff like that. She is not at all selfish or anything, she really shares.' There was an answering service, and an answering machine, which the students checked when they were away. Becky and Kathy's quarters were self-contained, separate from Martina and Rita Mae's.

The house seemed gargantuan. Was it only twenty rooms? 'Oh shit, I don't know how many rooms it was, too many,' says Rita Mae. 'I had two graduate students from UVA, they could do some things, but I still had to run it.' A black woman came in to do some of the cooking and to clean. It was, after all, Virginia. Martina herself wasn't much help. 'Well, she didn't know how. All she knew was how to play tennis, besides which she was so physically exhausted from her work you couldn't expect her to do something like that. It wouldn't be fair.'

At first, in front of Rita Mae's witty, literary friends, Martina hardly spoke. The idea that her English was faulty was dispelled while they were watching a television programme about Jewish history called 'Masada'. At one stage the Romans were throwing Jews over the battlements in huge catapults, and Martina said, in a quiet ironical tone of voice, 'So that's what they mean by live ammunition.'

Words were a very important part of that life.

Thus it was on one of those long, sultry Virginia evenings that a joke-telling competition was held to see who could tell the worst dirty jokes. Rita Mae's feminist credentials were impeccable; so were those of the two female graduate students. Adam's enlightenment was accepted too. Martina was a fellow traveller. Therefore, 'You could make the most demeaning joke, in the worst possible taste, but you would be making it in inverted commas,' recalls Adam. 'You were so pure you could say anything and not be thought culpable.' That was the Good Old Gal in Rita Mae. It was also the intelligent free spirit. Rita Mae was the last woman in the world to fall prey to political rectitude if it reined in wit. She was, thus, a good teacher for Martina.

In the joke-telling competition, for which there is many an ancient literary precedent, there was a slew of jokes that were intentionally disgusting, but Martina's was pretty innocent. By all accounts, she told it well. The men in America, Martina began – not in these precise words – were being asked who they would most like to sleep with, who was the woman of their dreams. Everyone gave pretty standard answers, mainly the usual array of film stars: Marilyn Monroe, Bardot, Raquel Welch – this was the 1980s, remember. But there was one man the interviewers spoke to who kept mentioning a woman nobody had ever heard of, who was, he said, just unbelievable in her sexual attractiveness and power. Her name was Virginia something or other. It sounded Italian. As far as the researchers could make out, Virginia Pipileeni, or maybe it was Pippilinne, wasn't a film star or a sports person or any other sort of celebrity. They went to visit the man to do a follow-up interview, and it turned out that he had read about her in the paper. Ever since she had been the object of his fantasy. Eventually, he showed them the article. The headline read, 'Ten Die Laying Virginia Pipeline'.

The story works better when you tell it aloud.

The red clay of Virginia has the same terracotta colour as the crushed-clay courts on which Martina had played her first tennis. If Prague was, psychologically speaking, a million miles away, Revnice, the village in which she grew up, was at least a trillion. Despite the distance, walking, poking your shoe into the Virginia mud, it would be impossible not to think sometimes of the burnt, crushed clay of tennis courts. Although Virginia mud is springier underfoot than a clay court, it was practically the only thing in the vicinity of Flordon that would remind you of tennis. The house was not a shrine to Martina. Her tennis trophies were confined to the gym; so were her drums, a full set, big bass drum, snares, cymbals. Martina mostly avoided the gym, which was located in the bowels of the house. Occasionally on these summer nights she would go into the gym, very late, and beat out a basic rhythm, endlessly repetitive, mournful. Perhaps it was a form of aerobic frustration-release.

The gym had plenty of space for the full set of universal gym equipment and the drums in the corner. For the time, it was lavish for a private house, though not for the private house of a world-class athlete. One had no sense of tennis being an obsession in the household.

Martina practised on the university public courts, or health club courts, says Adam. 'I remember somebody saying how embarrassing it was to be doing your best to play a tennis game on Saturday morning and looking over and realizing that Martina Navratilova was on the next court.'

*　　*　　*

From the terrace, Martina could see clouds skating across the blue southern sky. 'Summertime and the livin' is easy', the song goes. But was it easy? They were giving parties and she was surrounded by people. Lately, however, Martina seemed to be in a world apart. She was living the fuller life Rita Mae advocated, but she was beginning to long to be elsewhere, high in the invisible range of sporting mountains.

A bestselling novelist, who had also done film and television work, Rita Mae had a fair amount of money; perhaps as much or nearly as much as Martina. Flordon, too large for them, was not a place either woman would have run on her own. 'I wish I had stayed at the farm,' says Rita Mae. Martina was not the only one who sometimes wished to be elsewhere.

Life with Rita Mae meant putting a lot of energy into being droll and charming. They were lavish entertainers. Southern hospitality and Czech hospitality are very similar, you always take very good care of your guests. Once they had about twenty friends over for a blind champagne tasting. It wasn't a vulgar occasion, it grew more from the conviction that everyone should drink champagne at times of celebration and know how to order the best instead of the most expensive. At the party, impecunious friends had a chance to decide if there was one they liked better than any other. The labels and the bottles were hidden but were numbered. There were forms where you indicated your verdict on a scale of ten. It was instructive. Nobody, it turned out, actually preferred the most expensive bottles.

Many of their guests were writerly academics from the university. There was nothing wildly counter-cultural about the parties, no lesbian demi-monde, although by Virginia standards the parties may have been bohemian.

They were not frequented by tennis people. 'We were off the beaten track.' Billie Jean and Rosie Casals and the others wouldn't have found it convenient to visit – had they wanted to – because it was at least three hours' drive from the site of the Washington Virginia Slims competition.

The tennis player in the jeans and jeans jacket who said very little and rarely used her private gym was a shadowy presence in the house. At social occasions, she would often be in the background. In that crowd, she didn't seem that sure of herself socially. But once she started talking, she projected an ease of being with herself that people who met her noticed and that you didn't get in the interviews on television.

At one party they gave, Rita Mae hired Adam to play the piano. They took the trouble of moving the piano out of the house on to the terrace. 'She gave me fifty bucks to play cocktail piano at one of her parties, not because I was a good cocktail pianist but because she could say, my pianist he's a novelist too. She liked that, she liked putting on the style.' That night, as 'Some Enchanted Evening' rang out over the rolling Virginia hills, Martina stood in the background, as she usually did at these parties. She was becoming less and less enchanted. Fortunately it was time to be off on the tour. Martina took Rita Mae with her to Wimbledon. That Martina was bisexual or lesbian was not yet public knowledge. The press, however, were beginning to get a whiff of scandal.

It was a farce, a series of chase scenes in a Laurel and Hardy movie, but from Martina and Rita Mae's point of view, it soon became a horror movie. The photographers from the tabloids keeping them under surveillance were utterly relentless and shameless, as were the reporters from the *Sun*, who spent days doorstepping their flat near Sloane Square in London. They rang the champion's doorbell at seven in the morning even on those days she had a late afternoon match. Sleeping late, staying calm, hanging loose, which is desirable on match days, was made impossible.

Black humour was provided by the photograph of Rita Mae coming out of a grocery store with the caption 'Writer shops for love nest'. Martina was annoyed, especially since it was she who did most of the cooking. Throughout this ordeal neither acknowledged that they were a lesbian couple. Rita Mae was out of the closet, but her relationship with Martina was supposed to be simply business and friendship. One paper quoted Martina as saying, 'I find it offensive and ridiculous that anybody should think that I am gay.'

Besieged by the tabloid vultures in 1980, Martina found it hard to focus. Wimbledon was horrible that year, all rainy weather except on the day she faced Chris Evert in the semi. Martina won the first set, God knows how, and was winning the second when Chris hit a lucky shot that clawed at the net and somehow purred over. That shot, which wounded Martina's concentration, was the turning point of the match, which Chris won 4–6, 6–4, 6–2. It was for Martina a tremendous loss.

But at least it was over. She had probably never been so glad to leave Wimbledon. The US Open lay ahead. But Martina felt much less desire than usual to resume her training, much less inclination to face the piranhas of the press who might be waiting for her at Flushing Meadow. Perhaps not surprisingly, she failed even to reach the quarter-finals of the US Open, losing to the young Czech Hana Mandlikova in straight sets 7–6, 6–4 in the fourth round. The previous two years she had been the Wimbledon champion and made the semis at the Open. Now she seemed only to be losing. With the demise of Martina's tennis fortunes, a break with Rita Mae came closer.

As she strolled in the grounds of what was supposed to be their house, but which seemed somehow to everyone to be more Rita Mae's, Martina sensed that her tennis was going down the tubes, while Rita Mae was telling her not to worry, there was more to life than tennis. But whether or not Martina was quite ready to admit it to herself, it was beginning to be apparent that she would have to break with Rita Mae. The easiest way to leave one lover is to find another; in time, Martina would do just that, and she would do it again and then again.

The grounds for leaving Rita Mae were not just personal, nor did they have a great deal to do with the terrible publicity their relationship was causing and the fortune Martina would lose thereby; nor with the fact that the relationship was homosexual.

Sure, it probably had something to do with all that, but the main reason for the split was profoundly and impressively professional.

There had been an important private complication to the relationship, a very unpleasant visit from Martina's mother Jana and her stepfather Mirek, who had emigrated to America in December 1979. Martina had bought her parents a house in Texas on the same street as the one she had. But they did not like living in America, where they had trouble with the language and where they discovered that Martina had grown up. They wanted to live in the same house as she did, to return to the old days when she did what they said. But Martina was now twenty-three years old.

When they fathomed Martina and Rita Mae's relationship, they did not take it well. In April 1980, she told them she was buying herself a second house near Charlottesville. Later, they visited her and Rita Mae there, and in the midst of what Martina calls 'a raging argument', the mother and stepfather revealed that Martina's real father – dead a dozen years – had committed suicide. He had killed himself because of an unhappy love affair, because he cared too much for women. Warning Martina that she had the same manic-depressive, impulsive nature as her father, her mother predicted that if she didn't overcome her ardour for women, her life too would end in suicide.

Her mother's words, which must have hurt so much, would ultimately help transform Martina into a great champion. Her first success had come because she was trying to reclaim her maternal heritage, stolen by the communist government. Now her greatest success would come as she tried to elude her paternal heritage. Over and over, she would need to prove to herself and to the world that she could tempt fate and survive, she wouldn't commit suicide and she could not be killed by publicity, by envy, by the love or betrayal of a woman – or by sudden death on the tennis court. But for now, her parents' words just hurt.

97

Rita Mae arrived home about three hours later. 'Martina was stunned,' she recalls. There wasn't anything she could do about it. 'Done is done. She didn't know her real father very well and of course I certainly never did so I couldn't offer any advice. I could only offer a shoulder.'

Martina's mother pulled herself together and became fairly good about their relationship. Not the stepfather. He blamed the United States for Martina's sexuality. 'He was just very disenchanted with America,' says Rita Mae. 'There wasn't anything in America that he liked. So the fact that she was gay was yet another thing that was wrong with America. He was not pleasant to be around at that time.'

'Was he rude?' I asked.

'They have different manners than we do. That's a difficult question to ask a Virginian. You have to realize we think anybody north of the Mason–Dixon line is rude. So he seemed not very well-mannered to me.'

Martina seemed to recover from the trauma visited on her by her parents, but ever after, somewhere in the recesses of her mind, surely their rejection of Rita Mae as a suitable partner lay there between Martina and Rita Mae, a time bomb under the pillow. It may well have been a factor in their eventual break-up.

It would take till the following summer for Martina to figure it all out and pull Nancy Lieberman out of a hat. Actually, she met her in the press room of a tennis tournament. To this day Rita Mae Brown believes Martina left her for Nancy, which is, of course, true. But really, down deep, the other woman was tennis. No matter who her partner was, Martina would always have another mistress, Tennis. And Martina had been neglecting her.

Nancy, the next important woman in Martina's life, would say irately that Rita Mae wanted Martina to give up tennis and become an architect or a lawyer. Although Rita Mae denies that she suggested any specific career, she does admit there was

Plump and plucky. Winning in her first match at her first Wimbledon in 1973. (Michael Cole)

Facing page:
*Never afraid to go for
it. Eastbourne, 1979.*
(Michael Cole)

Left and below:
*Champion at last –
Martina enjoying her
first Wimbledon in
1978, as her friend
Chris Evert gracefully
accepts defeat.*
(Michael Cole)

1979 was another year to remember. Martina witnessed her second Wimbledon singles triumph and the historic doubles win with Billie Jean King. Jana Navratilova, pictured kissing Martina, had not seen her daughter for four years before Wimbledon fortnight.
(Press Association/ Topham)

Sandra Haynie, the golfer who taught her to be a champion.
(Hobbs Golf Collection)

The novelist Rita Mae Brown would help form one of the most interesting minds and the best sense of humour in tennis.
(Johnson/Frank Spooner Pictures)

That characteristic tearful resolve seen in defeat at the 1981 US Open final, where she lost to Tracy Austin
(Michael Cole)

The start of something wonderful – victory at Wimbledon in 1981 for the famous and fabulous doubles partnership of Martina and Pam Shriver.
(Michael Cole)

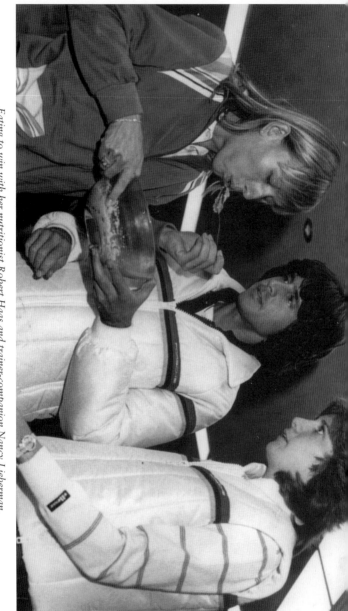

Eating to win with her nutritionist Robert Haas and trainer-companion Nancy Lieberman.
(Michael Cole)

an anti-tennis impetus. 'She had to make the decision, OK, what am I gonna do, am I really gonna learn about the world and be a more well-rounded person, or am I gonna be single-minded and dedicate myself solely to tennis, which I've done since I was eleven? And she made the decision to stick with her tennis for which we're all vastly entertained and grateful, but I don't know if it was the right decision or not, and she probably won't know until she's sixty. But it's the decision she made, and God bless her for sticking by it.'

At the time, though, Rita Mae did not feel so mellow about the decision. The break-up would be anything but mellow. Things had been going downhill with Rita Mae for some time. Martina was worried about her tennis. Her head was awash. She was full of indecision. What she needed at the moment was someone to tell her what to do. That person would be the red-haired basketball star Nancy Lieberman.

— 7 —

Denial Season

Although they had not yet decided to part, Martina did not take Rita Mae with her to Florida to the Amelia Island tournament that April, 1981. One night at Amelia Island, Martina had a dream. She was playing Chris and her side of the court was a valley, while Chris's was a mountain. With even the geography ranged against her, Martina was losing. It was at this tournament that she met Nancy. It was infatuation at first sight.

Martina first saw Nancy Lieberman across a crowded tennis court. Martina was in the middle of a match when she noticed the woman with flaming reddish-orange hair. 'I had always thought of female basketball players as burly and muscular, but she was slender and graceful.' They talked football and baseball and fell in love, but nobody was supposed to know about it.

Despite the distraction Martina managed to reach the Amelia Island final where she was playing Chris Evert. 'That match,' in April 1981, says Chris, 'was the first time I met Nancy Lieberman, who Martina got together with that week.' The match was not the most important in the world to Martina, but it was important to Chris who was the new touring pro at the Amelia Island tennis resort. Trying to make an impression in a new milieu, she beat Martina 6–0, 6–0. In eight years on the tour, this was the first time Martina had been bageled in a match.

Martina's tennis was again at a nadir anyway, and she may well have contemplated losing, but not to zero. 'Losing to Chris in the finals that way was shattering,' she admitted. Martina was not happy about it, but Nancy Lieberman was appalled. 'That was disgraceful,' Nancy was heard telling Martina. 'You should have more pride in your performance.' Two years younger than Martina, Brooklyn-born Nancy could be very direct. If what Martina needed was a kick up the ass, she had the perfect perpetrator. 'To get the best out of your potential,' Nancy told Martina, 'you're going to have to work hard and train hard.'

Nancy meant marine-boot-camp hard. Maybe harder.

The women's basketball league folded, and Nancy came to realize that there were no advertising spots or secure TV commentary positions for former basketball stars if they were female. Needing a new role, she became Martina's trainer. Publicly, that was all she was.

'I think that in a sense she was living through Martina, channelling everything into her because her own basketball career had ended,' Chris said. Whatever the reason, Martina was beginning really to get back into shape and enjoying her life again.

She also began to use her money differently. Not to buy baubles or culture, but to buy the support system she needed for her game. Renee Richards, who had made history as the first transsexual tennis player, honed Martina's strategy and boosted her self-confidence, teaching her to win even on off-days. Richards was also a calming influence. Martina, who had been training exceedingly hard since she took up with Lieberman, was building muscles. Renee and Nancy didn't always agree as to what was best for Martina. There would be a string of coaches and a nutrition expert, Robert Haas, who used a computer to work out his diets and whose diet for Martina became a bestselling book, *Eating to Win*. The 'nitwit nutritionist' Richards called him, but the diet utilized the then new wisdom of eating fresh fruit, only a little white meat and as a mainstay complex carbohydrates like pasta and potatoes. Haas concocted fruit bars for her to eat during matches.

There were jibes about Martina the bionic woman, the computer product, the 'robot'. 'The computer can't hit forehands for you,' was Martina's answer. 'I'm the one who has to go out there and run, lift weights, play basketball, whatever.'

In every aspect of her life, Martina valued expertise and wanted information. As Billie Jean King says, 'Martina was always on the cutting edge, Martina wants to know.'

On 5 May 1981, the Billie Jean King alimony scandal struck. It would have great impact on Martina's approach to making her own sexual orientation public. Marilyn Barnett, who had been Billie Jean King's lover, filed suit for what was called 'galimony'. Billie learned of the lawsuit in Florida, pondered it in New York, and flew to Los Angeles for the press conference where she would say, 'Yes, I had an affair while I was married, and it was with a woman.' Suddenly, Billie Jean King found herself the target of the biggest media blitz she had encountered since the Bobbie Riggs match. This time it was hard to be a winner.

'If I had been caught making love to a male movie star at high noon in Times Square, it wouldn't even have made the six o'clock news,' she mused in *The Autobiography*, 'but Billie Jean and a woman . . .'

The lesbian 'taint' had long shadowed tennis and golf, indeed sport itself. As Martina would point out again and again, up to and including her last Wimbledon, 'They don't ask who the gay men on the circuit are. But they ask the women players which players are gay.' One reason for this may be that the largely male sporting community may identify with the male stars and therefore find it difficult to ask questions about their sexual orientation. There are lesbians on the tennis circuit. There are, no doubt, lesbians everywhere. Even in the staid 1950s, 28 per cent of women admitted to Kinsey researchers that they had sexual responses to other women. Thirteen per cent had had sex to the point of orgasm. Forty years of openness towards sexuality has been going on since then.

Martina says that in the 1990s, about half a dozen of the top hundred tennis players are lesbian. 'I could go over the top hundred, and one year there may be five lesbians, one year there may be ten.' She is still the only one who has come out of the closet. In her autobiography, Billie Jean King presented her relationship with Marilyn Barnett as an interlude in what was overall a heterosexual life.

Another reason reporters went around looking for lesbians in the changing room then (and a reason why some still do) was that it seemed masculine and *unnatural* to them for women to play sport. But because sport is seen as an affirmation of manhood, no one reflects on a sportsman's sexuality. The discovery that Big Bill Tilden, the hulking Mr Tennis of the 1920s, was gay, and more recent revelations by American sportsmen, did not make many people regard the macho sportsworld with suspicion. There are apparently some present-day male tennis players who are gay but nobody pays much attention.

Sport has always been and still is to a very large extent viewed as masculine and masculinizing territory. For quite a long time it was thought in some circles that you had to be a lesbian to be interested in it. And if you were not, sport would by some alchemy – the slap of sneakers on the track, the sight of naked breasts in the changing room – 'convert' you. This view is fading. It is possible, though, that there has always been a higher proportion of lesbians in sport than in the general population because it took a certain amount of disregard for convention for a woman to admit to homosexual feeling, and it was unconventional for a woman to put her body on the line at elite sport. For years, too, the fear of being thought lesbian has kept some heterosexual women out of sport.

With a battery of lawyers, Billie Jean King and her husband Larry won the law case in the courts. Marilyn Barnett, the ex-lover, who had travelled the circuit as Billie's secretary-companion and who was now confined to a wheelchair, had wanted a share of the riches Billie Jean King now had. The Kings' careful presentation of the case to the media and the public, who in America can forgive almost anything if you own up and don't seem terminally embarrassed, helped. Many of Billie's chief fans were feminists and in the United States then that included most female high-school graduates and their cookie-baking housewife mothers. Billie Jean King felt she was on a tightrope and she walked it carefully. Gloria Steinem, the respectable voice of American feminism, wrote to her, expressing sympathy at the fact that she had to bare her private life in public: 'It's not fair that you were forced into this position – but now that it's happened, I think some good will come of it.'

Billie estimates that in addition to walloping legal fees, the case cost her at least one and a half million dollars (£1 million) in earnings. Bravely she said, 'In those few moments of a lifetime that Marilyn and I shared, she gave me a great deal. She was extremely important to me. And if she hadn't burned me, I would have no regrets. No, not for the love. None.' But she would always maintain that those 'few moments of a lifetime' – which had taken place over a year or so, or over seven years, depending on which version of the story you accepted – were a mistake, not a sexual preference. Thirteen years later, in the players' lounge at the French Open, she told me that she was still bisexual and explained the agony that for years had been preventing full disclosure. I believe that was the first time since the scandal that she had ever discussed the subject so freely with a journalist.

Martina would be more forthright, but not immediately. At first, she denied everything. Then she called a press conference to deny everything. What complicated the whole thing for Martina, just as it had for Billie Jean King, was money.

Ever since tennis had allied itself with a tobacco company, the sport had been wed to commerce. When the Women's Tennis Association, a go-getting, PR-conscious players' union, was formed by Billie Jean King and others in 1973, a large part of its brief was to make money for the players. And it has. Since 1975, there has been pay parity between the sexes at the US Open. The money in the sport has become enormous.

Tennis had plenty of money but was feeling the pressure of the lesbian scandal, and that put pressure on Martina. What was worrying Martina at least as much as what people in Richmond and Revnice would think was the effect a scandal would have on her endorsements and on her sport. The tour's interim sponsor, Avon, the cosmetics firm, was said to be leery. Women were marketed in sport on their *perceived* femininity. You had to be a winner to get an entry, but a petite, soft, well-dressed, pretty, white, feminine winner was the one likely to succeed in the sponsorship stakes. Very often, unless she was a complete turkey, hers were the matches that received the media coverage too.

This is slightly less true than it used to be. Sport is a tremendously conservative arena and sports writers as a group – with some very notable exceptions – do not like women's sports. In Western countries, even in Japan, many more women are now participating seriously in sport; more women have biceps, and to some extent the commercials have had to change – because the customer is always right. None the less, the Beauty of the circuit, Gabriela Sabatini, seemed to earn more endorsement money than the tabloids' Beast, Martina. The so-called prodigy Jennifer Capriati, who was perceived as a wholesome American teenager, made a million, even before she won anything. In fact, although she knocked out some big names at important tournaments, she never did win anything much. Martina would have her own galimony divorce scandal from Judy Nelson a decade later than Billie's. Meanwhile, she and Nancy Lieberman did the best they could.

Everyone had always been uptight about the lesbians on the tour. That was the supposed reason Rita Mae had been forced to stay away from what would have been her and Martina's last joint Wimbledon. In the midst of the fallout from the palimony scandal, Martina was worried about jeopardizing her American citizenship, which she had applied for six years earlier. The hearing was at the end of May 1981, less than a month after the palimony scandal broke.

In some states homosexuality is a crime. 'I was afraid my sex life could keep me from becoming an American citizen. If that happened, where would I live?' This was no paranoid delusion. For years, anyone entering the United States, even a tourist coming for a two-week holiday, was asked if he or she were homosexual. If the answer was yes, admission could be denied.

The press, fired up by the King scandal, renewed their attack on Martina. 'They started asking me, are you gay. I said I cannot talk about that because I'm trying to get my citizenship. I won't talk about that now, and it's none of your business, you shouldn't be asking that question, which they should not, because they do not ask male athletes who they know are gay. But women athletes are a prime target.' The press conference she and Nancy gave took place, however, after she had received her citizenship.

There was pressure from the sport to keep quiet. Nancy too seems to have wanted to be covert; not so much Martina.

'It wasn't something that was taboo with her,' Chris Evert says. 'If anything, sponsors and tennis officials would advise her to keep in the closet so to speak because it might hurt women's tennis.'

On the advice of her lawyers, Martina had filed her citizenship application in Los Angeles, where the climate was freer and easier than in Virginia, one of the states where homosexuality was illegal.

At the hearing, Martina had to write a sentence in English, name the first president of the United States, state the colours of the American flag, and the nature of her sexuality. 'I just gulped and said I was bisexual.'

The official asking the questions didn't bat an eye. It had gone like clockwork, but nothing was signed, sealed or delivered, nor would it be until the swearing-in ceremony a few weeks later. That delay left Martina slightly fraught. There was a great deal else happening in her life, including the French Open where she lost in the quarter-final, and Wimbledon where she lost in the semi in three sets to the brilliant but erratic Czech who had once been her ball girl, Hana Mandlikova. That was the year Chris Evert won her third Wimbledon. Martina's tally was still only two. And at that moment Martina must have doubted she would ever catch up.

Someone – was it Rita Mae? – had initiated Martina into the capitalist ritual of sending a bottle of champagne to commemorate splendid occasions. Martina had sent Chris champagne after some of her triumphs at the US Open. Now, in the face of everything, she did not omit the courtesy. Nor did she stop being sociable. 'After I won the 1981 Wimbledon singles title, Martina sent a complimentary bottle of champagne to my hotel room,' Chris recalled. 'I invited her to celebrate with John and me at Wimbledon. She came to our party and stayed the whole evening.'

In the climate in which it had happened, it was no wonder that Martina's break-up with Rita Mae was not as smooth as it might have been. In fact, it was a disaster. Rita Mae was the only out lesbian in any way associated with the tour, and from every point of view that was a great inconvenience.

Eager to be free and eager to be with Nancy, Martina had gone home to face Rita Mae, to tell her everything was over. The words one chooses at such moments are not the ones any of us would want to be judged on. And usually there are so many words, too many. Often the ones that stick in each partner's memory are different. 'I just said, I'm leaving. I've got to get my act together,' recalled Martina, the athlete, who would be shocked because she encountered physical violence. Rita Mae, the writer, would remember most what she perceived as violent words. 'She said, you're old, I don't want you any more.'

The scene that followed was not pretty. Break-ups rarely are. It had been a close, a deep relationship; its sundering hurt. 'We began fighting, shouting, crying,' Martina recalled in her autobiography. 'Let's say she did not take it lightly. She was hurt, anybody would be, and we got into one of the nastiest, most physical arguments I ever hope to be in.' They went from room to room, 'raging at each other'. Finally, 'I raced out of the house, getting into the car before she did, and I jammed it into gear and spun out of the driveway, spewing gravel and exhaust fumes, while Rita Mae stood in the driveway, gesturing at me.'

Martina had a licensed pistol she kept in the house for protection against prowlers. It had somehow come to the surface. Now, as the car door slammed on their relationship, Rita Mae happened to see Martina's pistol, and, needing something to throw, hurled it. 'I didn't realize the gun was loaded.' Rita Mae says that to her horror the gun went off. The ricocheting bullet shattered the back window of the car, missing Martina by inches. 'Ever since then I got real serious about gun control,' says Rita Mae. 'It scared the living daylights out of me.'

I asked, 'Rita Mae, did you shoot at Martina and try to kill her?'

'Oh no. If I were gonna shoot at somebody, I wouldn't miss. I have very, very good hand–eye coordination.'

Over the years, Martina and Rita Mae have resumed contact. Martina telephones. Rita Mae writes her letters. There are not many hard feelings now.

'Now we're all old enough,' says Rita Mae, 'that we can see patterns to people's lives and that's her pattern, that's how she renews herself, and there's nothing wrong with that. I think a new person in her life gives her tremendous energy and focus. She's found what works for her. Whether it will work after she leaves tennis, I don't know. I think about two, two and a half years, that's about her speed. That's what I've observed over time. She has to keep doing it, but every time she does it, it works. There's chaos and crisis for a while, and then she settles down and she's really happy, and she plays great.

'I also think it was a critical point in her life where she had to make that major decision' – as to what she would do with her life – 'and what easier way to make it than to find somebody new who's gonna help you make it, because, see, I refused to participate in that decision. It's not my life, I can't possibly make that decision for anybody, that has to come from within.'

Martina's practice of serial monogamy was no different than that of many others in the limelight. Scientists have recently documented not a seven-year but a three- or four-year itch, which is caused by human biochemistry. People who can afford to often move on. Martina moved on. As the anthropologist Margaret Mead once said of her own life, 'I have been married three times, and none of my marriages was a failure.'

On 20 July 1981, Martina and fifty or sixty other people recited the oath of allegiance. Then came the words Martina had been awaiting for years: 'I now pronounce you citizens of the United States.' She got her passport the very next day.

The citizenship scare was over, but it was still denial season. Martina told reporters that she couldn't say anything about her sexuality because it would hurt women's tennis, which was looking for a new sponsor. Then, in August, she and Nancy gave a press conference which by all accounts was astonishing. There were no longer legal reasons to hide her homosexuality, but there were still plenty of financial ones. The purpose of the press conference in Dallas was to stave off any rumours about her sexuality. There had been a lot of scandal-mongering in the British tabloids. But none of great moment in the United States. Under the libel laws in America, you could not call a person a homosexual unless they admitted it, or they could sue. Martina had not admitted it. Rita Mae always maintained that her relationship with Martina was strictly business. However, during a one-on-one interview with Steve Goldstein of the *New*

York Daily News, Martina said they were having a lesbian relationship. He had kept silent until after the citizenship hearing. Now he was preparing to publish. To Martina, however, it seemed the vipers were closing in. What she didn't realize was that one report could be denied – a public statement couldn't be.

At the press conference called to defuse the situation, Martina announced that Nancy, who was not known as a lesbian, was going to reintroduce her to a heterosexual lifestyle, the implication being that for a while Martina had fallen into bad company, Rita Mae's. The journalists in Dallas were astounded. This was Martina's first admission that she had ever had a lesbian relationship. She had admitted she was, at the very least, bisexual. The press conference had exactly the opposite effect it was intended to have. Now the media could call her lesbian or bisexual with impunity. This was the reverse of what she had intended.

Not until Judy Nelson's arrival on the scene in 1984, three years later, would it no longer seem worth the trouble to lie. Denial season would end for practical purposes, and also, no doubt, for political ones. 'Although I know my candour about my sexuality has cost me millions of dollars in sponsorships and endorsements, that's only money. I play my heart out on the tennis court, and that's what people want from me. Could I play as well if I were living a lie?'

After Martina left, Flordon must suddenly have seemed very big to Rita Mae. What happened next cannot be called a nervous breakdown. It was much more in control than that, but for Rita Mae it was a bad time. Once she had palpitations and other symptoms that suggested a heart attack. Becky accompanied her to a hospital emergency room but it wasn't the treatable sort of heart attack, the trauma was emotional.

Becky's job had temporarily changed from that of house attendant to something bordering on nurse. For a time, Rita Mae just didn't want to be alone. At night, Becky would sleep in her bed. It wasn't sexual in any way. When Adam Mars-Jones arrived for a short visit, he too found that Rita Mae needed the solace of companionship. They slept three in a bed. 'It was a big bed so it was not as intimate as it might seem.' It was a bit like a children's slumber party, although the conversation was wittier. Until they fell asleep, they just chatted or made faces at the mirrors on the ceiling. Even depressed, Rita Mae was talkative and good company, but it would take her a long time to get over Martina.

Rita Mae always liked to talk about ovaries as an analogy of the way one talks about men having balls. She used to say as a term of approval, 'That woman has ovaries coming out of her ears.' She felt that women needed a jocular, strong and unsentimental way of talking about strength. She also talked about ovary-busters and ovary-busting, an analogy to ball-breakers and ball-breaking. At the time, a distraught Rita Mae told a few people, who believed it and certainly believed she thought it true, that Martina's first female lover, a tennis player who was older, had 'busted Martina's ovaries'. In other words broken her heart, and ever since then, she believed, Martina had been breaking everybody else's ovaries.

A couple of years later, the woman scorned would recover enough to publish the novel *Sudden Death*, which many reviewers regarded as a *roman à clef* to the tennis scene. In other words, the fictional characters were recognizable in life. One of the protagonists was a female university teacher who lived with a South American female tennis player, whose character was in some ways similar to Martina's. The antagonist was called Mrs Susan Reilly, an old pro, who had a husband she didn't sleep with and a female lover. To this day Rita Mae denies it was a *roman à clef*.

But as Martina would say in 1994, anticipating the publication of *The Total Zone*, the tennis mystery novel she herself had 'co-written', 'It's fun writing fiction because, number one, you can't get sued, and you can trash people and they know who they are.'

8

Doubles Trouble

'Billie Jean King doesn't like you,' I mention to Rita Mae. 'I'm sure I'm not telling you anything you don't know.'

'Well she's missing a good thing.'

'Can you figure out why she didn't like you?'

'I think at that time she feared they'd worked so hard to get the women's tour independent and they didn't want to be associated with anything feminist at all, and they associated me with the feminist movement. I believe that Billie Jean thought I was gonna try to politicize women's tennis, which of course is impossible. I couldn't do it if I tried.'

'Billie Jean King thinks that you told Martina to drop her as a doubles partner.'

'Oh Billie,' Rita Mae titters, 'she must be smoking opium. Martina's tennis was her business, it wasn't my business.'

'Billie says you told Martina that every time they won at doubles it would raise the record and it would be harder to overtake Billie. As a kind of a pre-emptive strike you told her she should break up the team. Is that true?'

'No, I don't think like that.'

'Well it is thoughtful, we have Martina the impulsive person who doesn't think ahead, so it has a certain ring of credibility to it. There's nothing criminal in it if it's true.'

'No. I don't know why she left her. I think doubles partnerships are like any other partnership. There's a point where it's not as productive any more. She didn't talk that much about it but when she got ready to go she said, who do you think is good, and I listed a couple of players, and I said, well they're young, they're kinda your age. See how it works. So she picked Pam. I didn't meddle in her career, that's not my business.'

'Pam was on your list of top doubles players, was she?'

'Oh yes, she was on everybody's list.'

In October 1980, Martina made her decision, telephoning Pam Shriver, who was playing at a tournament in south Florida near Del Ray Beach. 'It was the first time I'd ever had a call from her. I had played with Betty Stove against Billie Jean and Martina in the finals of the US Open that year, played a good match, and she was looking for another partner so she called me up and asked if I could start playing the beginning of eighty-one. Needless to say I said yes. It was the luckiest break of my career. So from January eighty-one through the summer of eighty-nine we played doubles together.'

They lost their first tournament. 'We won the second one and lost maybe two or three matches that first year together, maybe the same the second year.' In 1983, they began their unparalleled two-year, 109-match winning streak.

Long before the start of the fabled winning streak, though, people were sitting up and taking notice. One of them was Judy Nelson, who met Martina when she and Pam were playing doubles at Fort Worth in 1982. But I will get to that. The Navratilova–Shriver team's first big win was the year before, at the very first grand slam the new team had played – Wimbledon, in 1981. In the finals they beat the defending champions, Smith and Jordan.

One thing everybody noticed was that they were always talking. What did they say to each other on court?

Pam chuckles at the thought of it. 'Some you couldn't repeat. A lot of times, we were winning so easily, if we said stuff or talked on changeover, it wasn't even necessarily about the

113

match. But other times, if it was a close match, we would talk strategy and how to try and figure this situation out.'

'And if you lost, did you blame each other?'

'Nah. We were really a good thing. That was the best part – we never did any of that. She took a lot of pressure off me and vice versa.'

'What was the secret of the team?'

'Well, we did all the things that you do naturally as a good doubles team. We were the lefty-righty combination which is good because it was always different. Your opponents never got used to a certain spin on a serve, they were catching it different ways every time. It worked for us. Most of the time I played the right side of the court. Our backhand volleys were in the centre, which worked well for us because our backhand volleys were our better volley. And we just clicked. We had good chemistry. We were both quick with our hands which is always important.

'I tended to do the basics more, to stick to high percentage, solid doubles stuff,' says Pam modestly, 'and she tended to come up with some outrageous stuff, lower percentage but a lot of times it came off and worked for her.'

Martina immodestly agrees. 'Pam was the steady one, I was running around hitting angled shots.'

'One reason we were so good we always knew where the other person was on the court.' There was very little bumping into each other. But there were funny moments. At the Australian Open it just rained and rained, and the fans and the players, who had to sit there waiting for the rain to stop so they could play, were miserable. Rita Mae was dispatched to hire some scuba-diving gear including big, floppy fins. When play began, Martina and Pam arrived on the damp court wearing them. To the delight of the crowd, they even hit a few balls while wearing them.

The 109-match winning streak, which lasted over two years – from 23 June 1983 to 9 July 1985 – finally came to an end on Wimbledon Centre Court.

A few hours after Martina's arduous 4–6, 6–3, 6–2 triumph over Chris Evert in the singles, she and Pam lost the 1985 doubles final 5–7, 6–3, 6–4, to Kathy Jordan and Liz Smylie. Until then, Martina and Pam, the Wimbledon champions since 1981, had won eight successive grand slam titles. It was a staggering defeat. The moment they shared together afterwards in the locker room was full of emotion. They felt very sad and very proud. 'We both had a little bit of a cry,' recalls Pam, 'and yet we had this great realization of what we had accomplished together over two years – to have not lost. We patted each other on the back and said, this probably won't be beaten, this streak, no one may ever do this again.'

Martina showed her resilience by going on to win the mixed doubles in yet another three-setter, 7–5, 4–6, 6–2. Her partner was the Australian Paul McNamee. It had been an emotionally and physically exhausting Wimbledon for Martina. At the Champion's Dinner, she said, 'When I got into the bath after the mixed was over, I didn't want to get out of it again.'

The Navratilova–Shriver doubles team would win a total of twenty grand slams, the last at the Australian Open in 1989. Then, Martina ended the partnership. Pam wishes she hadn't. 'I was sorry that at a couple of US Opens – two, both in eighty-nine and ninety-one – Martina chose to play with somebody else, because we were tied with Louise Brough and Margaret Osborne for twenty grand slam titles – the all-time record the other team set thirty-two years earlier – 'and I believe we would have won one or both of those. I know we would have won one.' The break-up of the partnership prevented Pam Shriver from attaining what would have been her only all-time record. 'In eighty-nine Martina won with Mandlikova,' says Pam, 'and they beat Mary Joe and myself in the finals.' Not only had Mary Joe Fernandez never before been in a grand slam final, it was the first tournament she and Pam had ever played together. Hence, Pam thinks that partnering Martina, she certainly would have won. 'I was playing good doubles. I was having trouble with my singles, and I was having a little trouble with my head, but my doubles was solid and good. We would have won that US Open.'

'You think she should have hung in there for you?'

'Yeah, I felt in the middle of the summer she shouldn't have bailed me in the ninth. But that's OK. We had over eight straight years of a partnership so if it has a hiccup every eight years that's not too bad. Again in ninety-one we had gotten back together. We played that year some, but she was defending US Open champion with Gigi [Fernandez], so I don't blame her for wanting to defend her title, and as it turns out I won the Open with Zvereva, which I'm very proud of, that was a great win for us, but I still would have liked Martina and myself to have won that twenty-first slam title. The only thing I really regret is that we didn't sneak in that twenty-first.'

'Any funny stories?'

'Well, yeah, the night we won our hundredth at Eastbourne in 1985. It was a party the WTA planned for us, there were about twenty of us. It was time for us to deliver a toast to the group and to each other, and Martina stood up first, and she said that I was the greatest partner she had ever had and she wanted to play the rest of her career with me, and it was amazing that we'd won a hundred in a row. So I took a little cocktail napkin and I wrote, when I heard her say I only want to ever play with Pam, I put I, Martina Navratilova, promise only ever to play doubles with Pam Shriver. I drew a line, I said signed, and then I put like another line, witnessed. So when she finished her speech I had this little napkin, contract, so I stood up to give my speech. And as I stood up, I found my head in one of these lampshades hanging over the table' – she mimes it, acts it out – 'so I stood up like this and my head just went inside the lampshade. I got the lampshade off and replied to Martina's toast and I brought out the paper, and she signed it, and I had George Hendon, the tournament director, sign it as the witness, and I still have it.'

'But you never took her to court.'

'No. I would never do that. Friends never do that.'

~ 9 ~

The Trophy Wife

Judy Nelson radiated a graceful passivity. Her face was a fault-less arrangement of well-appointed rather than gorgeous fea-tures. Tall, blonde, wholesome, statuesque, she was beautiful in the calm manner of an engine always at idle. In comparison with Rita Mae, Judy was less obviously clever. In comparison with Nancy, less aggressive. It was not immediately apparent in what way she would be a guru to Martina. Although eleven years older, Judy knew less than Martina about almost every-thing that up till now had been important in Martina's life. What she knew was how to belong.

Martina, the tennis nomad, the wild, imaginative one in the two-dimensional world of tennis players, had never quite belonged anywhere. Not in Prague where they had been aston-ished when the boyish one first appeared in the women's chang-ing room. Not at Wimbledon where her abrasive manners and foreignness did not commend her to the scions of the All England Club. Not in the quiet world of Haynie or the wordy, more intellectual one of Rita Mae. And Nancy, the ex-basketball player, had been absorbed, like a vitamin.

Judy Nelson was all that was best about White Anglo-Saxon Protestant (WASP) America. Judy was the very incarnation of respectability, not just a member of the country-club set, but also a doctor's wife. Martina had already lived with two women in Texas, Haynie the native and Nancy the New Yorker-turned-Texan. With Judy, Martina would again reside in the Lone Star State, but this time she would be admitted into what many regard as the 'best circles'.

Life with Judy Nelson seemed to promise Martina fulfilment, at last, of the American Dream. For what is that dream but fame, fortune and a blonde on your arm? In her youth, Judy had even been a beauty queen of middle rank, called Maid of Cotton.

Taller than Martina, buxom for an American beauty rose, she carried her height and her weight in exactly the same manner she would later carry off her admission of her lesbianism, elegantly. But Judy was a throwback. The old-fashioned, pre-feminist woman. There was nothing political about her lesbianism. She loved Martina.

They met through Judy's older son Eddie, then eleven, who was a ball boy at the Bridgestone World Doubles Champion-ships, which were played for the one and only time in Fort Worth in March of 1982. It would take two years of shilly-shallying before the first lunch date, after which Martina was invited to stay in the doctor's house. The Nelson marriage was already on the rocks. The doctor had been unfaithful, Judy said, and she believed strongly in monogamy. In 1984, his wife and Martina would begin their seven-year relationship. The Nelsons were the last sort of people you would have thought to take up with the lesbian tennis star. Was it her money? Was it her fame? Or did something in Judy tell her from the moment they met that she wanted to be close to Martina? In all the reams of information that has been written about their story, this ques-tion was never convincingly answered until Judy addressed it in *Love Match*, the book Martina tried legally to prohibit her from writing. Judy implies it was love at first sight and certainly believes it was fate. 'When I met Martina, I instantly felt a bond with her, that feeling that this person will be in your life for ever. It was a feeling. Unexplained. Accepted.'

In the beginning, Judy probably believed feminists were

bra-burners with hairy upper lips. As for lesbians, before her relationship with Martina, there was no reason for her view of them to be anything but stereotyped. Yet Martina exuded health, vitality. She was now in excellent physical shape. Judy was not the only one who noticed.

At the 1981 US Open, in a semi-final that was interrupted to remove brawling spectators, Martina had defeated Chris for the first time since the Amelia Island fiasco five months earlier. Nancy and Nancy's regimen were already having an effect on Martina. 'She was more consistent,' Chris noticed. 'She was playing better tennis, seemed in better shape, and was more hungry.' That didn't leave much out. That year, Martina finally reached the final of the US Open, which she lost 1–6, 7–6, 7–6, to Tracy Austin, whose victory was an act of will, combined perhaps with a failure of nerve on Martina's part. Tracy had been trounced in the first set; embarrassed to lose so badly on national television, she dug in to eke out a few points, and unexpectedly turned the tide.

'Near the end of our match,' she recalls, 'Martina started crying.' She had never won the Open. 'On match point she double-faulted. I don't think she could see through her tears.'

At the awards ceremony, Martina couldn't stop crying. Many in the crowd had been cheering for her. Perhaps that was partly why she was crying. 'I want to thank each one of you who was pulling for me today,' Martina said. 'I really didn't think that would happen.'

That Open would turn out to be Tracy Austin's last grand slam final; she would retire early because of chronic injury. Soon Martina would see off a generation of pony-tailed Tracys and Andreas, and then she would outlast the most well-known prodigy of all, Jennifer Capriati. Weak backs or weak will would claim them. Martina would lose a few important occasions, but by the summer of 1982 she had achieved the Roman ideal, a classical balance – she had a strong mind in a strong body. She would endure. Martina had not yet overcome her Waterloo, the US Open. It was evident, however, that one day she would.

At Wimbledon 1982, one of the wettest ever, Martina sailed to the final. 'I haven't been tested,' she said.

In the final, Chris would provide a very severe test. 'Nerves might be a factor,' Chris said, knowing hers were steely; and that Martina's weren't. But, down a break point in the third set, Martina stood up to the pressure and beat Chris 6–1, 3–6, 6–2. After two years in the heady oasis of Rita Maedom, Martina had returned to the simple life and won her third Wimbledon.

She went from strength to strength, and the following year, 1983, in a final held in 93-degree heat, Martina finally won her first US Open at her eleventh try. On that September day at Flushing Meadow, Ms Martina Navratilova in her prime – athletic, with her serve and volley game at its apogee – defeated Chris Evert almost easily, 6–1, 6–3. Chris was definitely on the run. Martina was already being recognized as perhaps her generation's finest player. 'If I don't win another tournament in my life,' Martina said, 'I can still say I've done it all.'

Talking strategy with Renee Richards had been a big help. Now Martina went into matches with a Plan A, a Plan B and even a fallback position, Plan C, in her head. There is no proof of the allegations that Renee, a medically trained doctor who had the right to write prescriptions, gave her anabolic steroids. This is an allegation made against most female sports stars in athletics – the fastest woman in the world, Flo Jo the sprinter, has had to put up with it, as has the javelin thrower Fatima Whitbread. Even the skinny female distance runners like Ingrid Kristiansen and Liz McColgan have been suspected of blood-doping or using other bio-chemical aids. The idea that women can work hard and win naturally is to some people anathema.

During the fifteen-minute chat they had had in the players' lounge in Fort Worth in 1982, Judy became aware of Martina's smile, her soft brown hair with its blonde highlights, and realized that 'her body was the best I had ever seen. It was not the sleek body that epitomizes the "southern beauty queen," but a slender, athletic body with well-defined muscles, smooth and tight.' To Judy, Martina had legs 'to die for', soft, flawless skin, and 'the prettiest hands I had ever seen'. Judy remembers the firmness of the handshake. She remembers everything about the moment, even what she was wearing when she met Martina, an orange silk blouse and blue gabardine trousers.

No, it wouldn't be Martina stealthily entrapping Judy, but now, for the first time, all those tabloid stereotypes seemed to be being realized. Judy was much older and two inches taller, but Martina did appear physically to be the masculine partner. There is absolutely no evidence that the butch–femme syndrome predominates in lesbian life, but belief in the stereotype is widespread, even among some lesbians. The fashions in the gay sub-culture change, just as they do in the rest of life. The gentle, child-rearing New Man is again on the wane; similarly, the egalitarian lesbian couple may be less common than it was during the period of the 1970s and early 1980s, when feminism held sway. Certainly, in Martina's relationship with Rita Mae, neither woman had been the 'wife'. And at the time she was with Martina, Nancy was definitely not wife material.

But in Judy, Martina had a woman who was used to being a wife. It was natural for Judy who, no matter what she argued in the law case, really had no profession that was more important to her than that of wife, to revert to that in her life with Martina. What she should have realized – because she had already had a husband who had strayed – was that wives become boring. This is perhaps one of the bitterest lessons of Western civilization.

Over the passage of time, this role was likely to lead to a diminishment of Judy's stature in Martina's eyes. There was also, of course, the even more bitter marital lesson, that 'this wonderful feeling' usually doesn't last. The rush of hormones which both partners feel in the early days of love, the anthropologists and biologists know now, levels off. Instead of this wonderful feeling, what remains is what you have in common. And contentment. And complacency. If you are a champion, you can't afford complacency.

Martina's tennis was at a high when she started her affair with Judy, and it continued wonderful. Some of her greatest accomplishments would happen during the Judy years. But many had happened even before they met. And when they got together in 1984, Martina was poised for one of the greatest accomplishments of her career. In 1983, she had won Wimbledon, the US Open (defeating Chris), and the Australian Open, and needed only to win the fourth grand slam event, the 1984 French Open, to capture what was called the Grand Slam. Only two women, Maureen Connolly in 1953 and Margaret Court in 1970, had done it previously. To purists, Martina's achievement over 1983/84 would not be a true Grand Slam because, although she won all four events consecutively, they were not all in the same season, but it was good enough for the International Tennis Federation, which would pay a million-dollar bonus.

Three months earlier, in March 1984, Martina and Judy met for lunch. Martina was in Dallas for the Virginia Slims tournament. She and Judy had been trying to get together since that first handshake but had never found a mutually opportune moment. Just as Martina had been trying to have tea with the Wimbledon prize-presenter, the Duchess of Kent, for years, so she had been trying to arrange lunch with Judy. Of course, the motives were rather different.

At the Wyndham Hotel in Dallas, both women ordered chicken salad sandwiches. Friends had asked Judy if Martina was gay. 'Beats me,' she said before the lunch. After it, she called a psychiatrist she knew and said, 'Either I'm going crazy, or I'm going to be the most interesting case you've had in a long time.'

That morning, in practice, Martina had pulled a hamstring – a serious and painful injury – which would prevent her from playing tennis for about a month. It was because she was injured that the Nelsons invited her to be their house guest. Friends counselled Martina to beware of becoming involved with a married heterosexual woman. Martina accepted Judy's invitation. Not at all a night owl, Martina sat up late into the night with Judy, after her husband and two sons had gone to bed, to discuss the practical complications of what they both were realizing was passion and soon would know was love. After about a week of these fervent conversations, Dr Nelson came home unexpectedly early one afternoon. Finding his wife sitting at the edge of Martina's bed, he fathomed the situation; and ordered Martina to leave. She moved into the nearby Green Oaks Inn where Judy went to visit her. Then, towards the end of April, her hamstring recovered sufficiently for her to play, she left for the tournament in Amelia Island, Florida.

Amelia Island was still Chris Evert's club. It was here three years earlier that Chris had bageled Martina; here that Martina met Nancy; here too that five years later she would decide to telephone Billie Jean King for help with her tennis. Now, with the new love in her life watching in the stands, Martina radiated confidence and joy. In New York in March Martina had defeated Chris Evert in the Slims final, a three-set agon; now, after a month's lay-off, which was not good, Martina pulverized Chris on clay, her best surface, and at her own club, 6–2, 6–0.

At the French Open, which is also played on clay, Martina greeted Judy with a pair of heart-shaped diamond earrings and a set of Louis Vuitton luggage. The earrings one can see as a symbol of their love, the luggage perhaps more a practical preparation for the nomadic tennis life on which Judy was embarking.

At the French Open final, on the outcome of which the million-dollar bonus was riding, Judy sat with Martina's parents in the players' box. Judy watched Martina crush Chris once again in straight sets, 6–3, 6–1. The Grand Slam was a deep notch in Martina the champion's pistol. Now she was really someone on the brink of immortality in tennis history. She felt, and was, golden. It is almost unimaginable for us mortals to comprehend how wonderful it must have felt. The world was at her feet, and she had Judy.

A million dollars richer, Martina flew to England for the pre-Wimbledon tune-up, the grass tournament at Eastbourne. Judy went home to Texas where she was greeted with a 'Welcome Home, Mom' banner draped between two trees in front of the house. Although she went to see her minister for counselling, she soon flew back across the Atlantic to Martina. Judy mentions seeing the final and then driving from Eastbourne to Wimbledon in a silver Porsche.

However, one ought not slough over Eastbourne. Millions are about to be spent updating and probably ruining it, but when Judy went there for the first time, Eastbourne was still the most wonderful, most traditional tournament in Europe, far nicer than Wimbledon. And it was very important to Martina.

Eastbourne didn't besiege you with bowls of fresh strawberries. There were no roving Becker groupies; no buzzing, burrowing crowds. But Eastbourne bore a distinct resemblance to a far finer Wimbledon, the cordial, tea-sipping Wimbledon of the mild-mannered past. Green stands and grass courts and serenity. Ivy climbing politely up the clubhouse wall. The Channel and an old-fashioned, elegant English pier are just ten minutes' walk away from Devonshire Park, where tennis has been played since 1870. The tennis crowd at these women-only championships is mostly female, of the sort who play a bit themselves, and whose tennis talk lingers on Anne Hobbs and Angela Mortimer's finest moments.

Only the ball girls had difficult opinions. The ones I talked to thought Martina beautiful; at that time she was. They would tell you too that fiery Hana Mandlikova stalked up and down the court when she came on, a territorial tic, but was sweet, and that Martina very rarely would accept new balls from the net; you had to send them down to the end.

Eastbourne immediately precedes Wimbledon on the calendar, is played on grass, and is still arguably the most important, solely women's championship in Europe, a breathing, perspiring Wimbledon form guide. Martina Navratilova, who had won here and then there since 1982, regarded Eastbourne as her own totem, a rabbit's foot in stadium form. Eastbourne where Martina defeated the American top-twenty player Kathy Jordan, 6–4, 6–1, was a better introduction for Judy to British tennisdom than frantic Wimbledon would be. But perhaps she preferred Wimbledon; it was more like Dallas.

That Wimbledon 1984 was another tremendously important tennis occasion. With a serve you could more than rely on, Martina triumphed over Chris Evert to win her fifth Wimbledon, 7–6, 6–2, in what was their sixtieth match. Up till now Chris had won more often than Martina. This was the match that brought them level, 30 to 30. No longer was Chris Evert's side of the court the summit of an unscalable mountain.

The tabloids expressed considerable interest in the blonde-haired attractive mother of two who was sharing Martina's rented house near Wimbledon. Judy, who says her hair was actually a Dallas tone of auburn, assured them that she and Martina were just good friends. There were journalists at the door at eight in the morning and at eleven at night. 'I didn't mind the questions,' Martina said. 'I minded the invasion of privacy.'

In the midst of Wimbledon Judy had made a thirty-hour lightning visit back to Texas to pick up her sons from summer camp. 'Are you gonna stay home now, Mom?' asked her younger son Bales, who was nine. The answer was no.

Judy explained that in fact she and Martina would be living together in a house that was being built for them in Fort Worth, not very far from the family's.

'Do you love Martina?' her thirteen-year-old, Eddie, asked.

'Yes, she is my friend and she makes me feel happy,' Judy said. 'I can even laugh again.'

It was at that first Wimbledon – very early days – that the lawyer's assistant whom some of the tabloid press mistook for

Judy, began to work on what would later come to light as the notorious agreement regarding the division of property should they part. Judy, whose husband gave no indication of failing in his child support, was already thinking of her future security. Martina would maintain she had thought BeAnn Sisemore was a legal adviser representing both of their interests. BeAnn, Judy says, was worried about her financial welfare if Martina died or left her. She explained that Judy needed a cohabitation agreement as well as a will, because she would have great trouble defending a will if Martina's parents chose to contest it.

'This marked the inception of the eventual partnership agreement,' says Judy. It was not, however, until two years later, on 12 February 1986, that BeAnn typed out a non-marital cohabitation agreement and Judy's brother Sarge videoed Martina and Judy signing it. Judy and Ed had been divorced nearly a year.

Martina and Judy were as houseproud as any other couple and were pleased to have their Fort Worth house photographed by the magazine *Architectural Digest*. The open-plan house, with its modern, over-sized furniture, was featured in 1986. The floor of the entrance hall had white marble squares intersected by black triangles, arcs and circles. A white lacquer dining table was balanced by a black Charles Rennie Macintosh willow chair. 'I told my interior decorator that I wanted black and white, a very Art Deco feeling,' Martina says. 'I love Art Deco. I'm a very visual person and I've always been interested in architecture. I love to walk around cities and just look.' The place reminded *Architectural Digest* of a Fred Astaire movie set.

There was no mention of Judy. It was described as Martina's house. Before buying this one, she explained, she had had a house in Dallas. 'Texas felt like home to me right away. I love the excitement of the East Coast,' she said, 'but here I have a sense of security, a feeling of home. I like the way people are so open and friendly.' Martina was photographed with the three dogs.

Judy says that when she started her life with Martina she gave up her acceptance by society, which she calls 'heterosexual privilege'. But Judy was not one to skulk around corners. Possibly because she was a WASP, she seemed to believe of the social world what Martina since childhood had felt about tennis; that it had been created to nourish her and help her flourish. Tennis was, remember, Martina's birthright. In Martina's autobiography published in 1985 there was a picture of Judy and the horse called Grand Slam she had given Martina for her twenty-eighth birthday. Martina, still hedging, mentioned in the book that she was bisexual.

Judy's parents supported her in what people referred to as her new 'lifestyle'. Her younger son wanted to be with his mother, but in the beginning of the relationship, Dr Nelson insisted that the grandparents chaperone every visit. Martina had arranged a condominium apartment near her and Judy's house where, so that they would not be inhabitants of the lesbian love-nest, the boys stayed with their grandparents. Later, things would loosen up considerably. There were constraints; there were difficulties; but from that summer of 1984 through about five of the next seven years, the living was easy.

As it happened, I had very distant family connections to Martina, which, like her grandmother Agnes Semanska's tennis glory over Vera Sukova, were at one remove. In 1985 or 1986, one of my brothers, a tennis fan, volunteered to pick up tennis royalty arriving for the Washington Virginia Slims. He was sent to pick up Judy Nelson and her father at the airport. 'They had a lot of bags, two dogs and a kid with them,' he says. That was Judy's younger son, Bales. They were bundled up for the Washington, D.C. winter weather, which was bitter. After he checked them into the hotel, my brother helped Judy's father carry up the bags. Sargent Hill, a big, bluff, democratic Texan wearing a hat akin to a Stetson, invited the young volunteer to join them for a drink.

The tournament was being held at George Washington

University. The players' locker room was the usual student changing room at the Smith Athletic Centre. After Martina's victory, the party was to be conducted to a little Italian restaurant at 26th and Pennsylvania Avenue. Judy and her father were ready to go and waiting for Martina. My sister-in-law-to-be Dianne, like my brother a graduate of the university, was dispatched to the locker room to fetch Martina. There she was shocked to see her standing amid the ordinary wooden benches and student lockers in a long fur coat. It looked like mink to Dianne. Fur was already *verboten* in the best East Coast circles in those days but evidently word had not reached Texas.

— 10 —

A Summer to Remember

The grey head nearly touches the bleached blonde one as ninety-year-old Kitty McKane Godfree, the oldest champion on the Wimbledon circuit, leans forward to press the famous Wimbledon silver plate into Martina Navratilova's big hands. If you were close enough, you could see the silvery plate reflected in Martina's glasses. It is the summer of 1986. Martina has just won her fifth consecutive Wimbledon title, becoming the first player ever to equal the more than half-century-old record of the temperamental Suzanne Lenglen. Kitty Godfree also witnessed Lenglen's fifth straight win, way back in 1923. Kitty Godfree herself won in 1924 and 1926.

Few of the 14,000 spectators at Centre Court that day doubted Navratilova's pre-eminence. Not only had she bested that other Czech, her former ball girl, Hana Mandlikova, 7–6, 6–3, in just 72 minutes, but at Wimbledon in the last five years Martina had lost only two sets. Now she had seven Wimbledon singles titles, one more than Billie, one less than the great Helen Wills Moody who held the record.

'I still want an all-time Wimbledon singles record which means winning it nine times at least,' said Martina.

Few present doubted her ingenuity either. Because the damp grass of the court was so slippery, Mandlikova changed her shoes twice during the match. Navratilova opted for more down-to-earth tactics. Soon after dropping service in the second game, she dispatched a ball boy to the kitchen for a fork, which she used repeatedly to scratch the soles of her shoes. This old-country ingenuity appealed to the British press. 'Sweet Martina,' the tabloid *Sunday Mirror* would say on the sports page, though elsewhere in the newspaper they continued to jibe her.

BBC television made much of the presence of Godfree, whom their commentator Dan Maskell, then seventy-eight, had actually seen win Wimbledon in 1924. Her silvery hair was tucked neatly in place under a hairnet, granny style, but in the conservative soft blue 'frock' she wore it was clear she had certainly not lost her trim, angular figure. Martina said that she wouldn't at all mind hitting some balls with Kitty Godfree, who even after a hip operation played doubles with her friends.

Godfree was a naturally bony, wiry type, not a curve on her; she had never ever been a dolly girl. Nor was weight training for women the fashion in Godfree's era. Navratilova, like the rest of today's female champions, used weights. She played as many matches in a season as Godfree and Lenglen would have played in five years. Until 1922, the defending champion at Wimbledon had a bye all the way to the final where she played whoever it was who had made it through the other rounds. In addition to the nineteen major tournaments Martina would play that season, she, like her contemporaries, played more minor exhibition matches.

You could see that the new champion's calf muscles bulged. The old one's calf, just visible beneath the hem of her soft blue dress, was straight as a willow, as it had been in her prime. The crowd had loved her stubborn, pursed-lip expression on court, and the dogged tenacity of her play when she defeated the American player, Helen Wills. At that Wimbledon, Wills would earn the nickname Little Poker Face, which as time went on became Miss Poker Face. Her cool manner annoyed the press and the crowd. 'There is no proof,' Wills said when forced to apologize for *not* losing her composure, 'that people do not become more calm at difficult moments than more nervous.'

Judy Nelson and her son at Wimbledon.
(Michael Cole)

Jana and Mirek Navratil with Martina in front of a poster of her at her old club, Sparta, in Prague, 1990. (Edwin Walter/Rex)

Facing page: *Facing down young Steffi Graf at Wimbledon in 1987.* (Michael Cole)

Fate defied. Martina during her 1990 Wimbledon triumph over Zina Garrison. (Michael Cole)

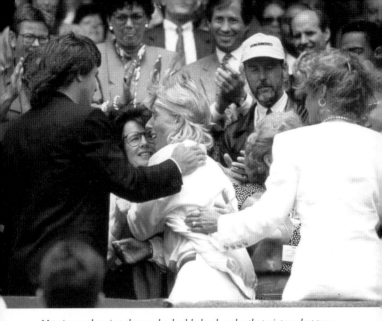

Martina embracing those who had helped make that victory happen: Billie Jean King and Judy Nelson. (Cris Barry/Action Plus)

At her last Eastbourne, the serve slower but still perfect technically.
(Anne McArthur)

Facing page: *In full flow: Wimbledon, 1992.* (Michael Cole)

With Conchita Martínez at the 1994 Wimbledon final.
(Glyn Kirk/Action Plus)

Decades later Chris Evert was derided on both sides of the Atlantic as the Ice Maiden. But image-making had by Chrissie's time become a paid professional art. Evert was transformed into an American Beauty (and, for a while, into a British wife) without changing her cool, methodical, merciless, baseline play. The Evert camp had done its best to melt the Ice Maiden image, and the sportswriters were gifted by the arrival of a new Beast, Martina. The beholders in the media didn't exactly change their storyline – they simply changed lenses, focused on a different aspect of Evert's character. Why? Partly because Evert had learned a few tricks of media management, partly because novelty is nearly everything in journalism and the Ice Maiden bit was becoming worn out, mostly because they needed a Beauty now that they had a new Beast.

'Martina feels very threatened by the fact that whenever we play the crowd is always on my side,' Chris Evert wrote in *Lloyd on Lloyd*. When Martina was retiring, Chris would analyze why they had liked her and conclude that it was because compared to Martina she was unthreatening. That may be so.

Helen Wills Moody, perhaps the greatest American player until Martina, was not as lucky as Chris Evert. 'The crowds never really liked Helen Wills and in all her years at Wimbledon,' Virginia Wade wrote in her history of women's tennis *Ladies of the Court*, 'there was not one time when they were really on her side. They always wanted her opponent to win.' Beauty is in the eye of the beholder. It would be a long time before the crowd as a whole began to will Martina to win, but that too would eventually happen.

Meanwhile she had another big occasion looming. After Wimbledon 1986, Martina would be returning to Prague for the first time since her defection. But can you ever go home again?

There was a light rain as the reliable party member Cyril Suk greeted the prodigal at the plane and accompanied her into the terminal where Martina's parents would be waiting. Suk, the father of Helena Sukova, the widower of Vera, a top Czech tennis official, behaved with perfect calm and decorum. Martina's then coach Mike Estep and his wife were arriving with her. Suddenly, Estep was very nearly knocked down, and Martina's mother felt a camera flashbulb go off in her face, as the shouting, shoving Western press did its best to cover the home-coming story.

There had been some fear that Martina would not receive the visa or would be turned away at the door, although the authorities had allowed the film director Milos Forman, who had left in 1969, back to film Mozart's story *Amadeus*. The countryside was green; the fruit trees heavy with promise; there were mushrooms dotting the fields near Revnice. It doesn't have the reputation for it, but the Czech Republic is a green and pleasant land.

Martina, who had led a Czech team to its first Federation Cup victory shortly before her defection, had returned as a player on the American team. The Federation Cup, played by 41 nations that year, is the women's equivalent of the Davis Cup. For the Eastern bloc it was a prime event, up there with the Olympics. The American team of Martina, Chris Evert, Pam Shriver and Zina Garrison had its practice sessions at Martina's old club, Sparta. There were no Martina posters on the walls – there are now – but they were glad to see her.

At the opening-day ceremony, as she listened to the Czech national anthem played by the Czech police band in Prague's new Stvanice stadium, there were tears running down Martina's cheeks.

Vlasta Vopickova was there with her children to hug her welcome. So was Jan Kodes, still a bigwig in Czech tennis. The fact that Martina was coming was not mentioned by the Czech media. But people knew. One woman, now a secretary at the Czech Tennis Federation, who came from Pilsen with her husband and three children to watch Martina play, said, 'It was not announced on the radio, it wasn't in the newspapers, or on the television. But at the tennis courts we played at, the director knew someone in Prague who had told him. So we got on the train and came.' Soon everybody knew. Czech newspaper readers probably realized that if it didn't say who was coming, it must mean Martina. They also had access to German and other foreign media. The crush of elated people at her every match was astonishing.

The only danger to the party was the young German Steffi Graf, who had beaten her on clay earlier in the year, and who was quickly becoming everyone's chief rival. There were those who said Martina owed her recent Wimbledon title to the virus that had struck Steffi in Paris and kept her from making much more than a social visit to Wimbledon. Now over the virus, Steffi was in Prague. There was relief among the home crowd when it was announced that Steffi, who this season had been somewhat accident-prone, had had a fight with a sun umbrella and come out the loser with an injured toe.

In a show of what may have been spite, officialdom put Martina on an outlying court for her first match, which she won. People were standing three, four, ten deep. When at last they put Martina on the model stadium Centre Court, built specially for the Federation Cup, each of the 7,500 seats was taken for the first and what would be the last time.

Hana Mandlikova was dismayed when the crowd applauded Martina's every point and applauded and applauded when Martina defeated her. The Czech crowd if it had ever disparaged Martina had now forgiven her. The Czechs accepted her as one of their own. America won the Federation Cup and the Czechs were elated.

Why did they prefer Martina to Hana? 'Forbidden fruit,' said Vlasta. 'Also she shows better sportsmanship on the court than Hana who gets angry.'

'Because she was forbidden we like her,' said the secretary who had come all those miles to see Martina. The Czechs are a strong-willed lot.

After Martina's last victory, a linesman who had known her

since she was a child came upon Martina in a corner weeping. He comforted her, and asked, 'But why are you crying?'

'I'm an American, a very rich American,' she told him, 'but I have a Czech heart.'

At the US Open a month later, the new girl, Steffi Graf, was gunning for her. High noon arrived at 3.57 on the clock, on 5 September 1986. As the sky darkened with the foreboding of rain, Navratilova, pre-eminent and just a month from her thirtieth birthday, stepped on to the Deco Turf court at Flushing Meadow to face the strapping, blonde, seventeen-year-old West German in the semi-final of the hundredth US Open.

All season, Graf, the sport's most talented newcomer, had been a giant killer – when she wasn't laid up with a virus or a broken toe. Navratilova had fallen to her in the German Open in the spring. Evert, Mandlikova, Sabatini, Sukova – they had all succumbed. On this symbolic centenary, Navratilova *vs* Graf was to prove a thrilling semi-final.

Many expected it to be the match of the decade: fine tennis and a foretaste of the impending future. They were proved right. Ignoring the black clouds and the heavy barometric pressure, Martina served and volleyed in her best manner, and hardly flinched when one of Graf's shots, bouncing strangely, knocked off her glasses. Graf defended with that powerful backhand, but Navratilova hit the winners, and when the rain came, in the first set, Navratilova led 4–1. On the next day, Saturday 6 September, Martina Navratilova gracefully finished off the set, taking it at 6–1.

In the second set, however, the story began to change. Although Graf broke early, and Martina kept on running to the net, Graf kept up the forceful forehand. And both players were everywhere; the tennis was enthralling. Stupendous shots: speed and power on the part of Graf, power and speed from Navratilova. With the crowd cheering the underdog all the way, it went to a nervous, sudden-death tie-break, which went to Steffi Graf. The second set was hers, 7–6.

Now both players were very tired, and both were playing well. Would the thirteen-year difference in their ages be the deciding factor? And if so, would it be trained stamina that would win, or youth? Was the balance of power in the tennis world about to shift?

The chaos and confusion and hyperactivity of the US Open has been compared to the running of bulls in Pamplona. That's something of an exaggeration. The US Open is the antithesis of Wimbledon. If Wimbledon is the apotheosis of class, the Open is the very incarnation of the seamiest aspects of egalitarianism. The one is elegantly uptight, the other disastrously hangloose. The Open is like Carnival in New Orleans or Notting Hill, with more noise, more crowding, less money in your pocket when you go home. The jets from nearby LaGuardia airport pass so low they muffle the server's grunt. Traffic noise doesn't help either, and the journey from Manhattan which takes about twenty minutes when there is no reason to get to Flushing Meadow can take an hour and a half when the tennis is on. Nor do New Yorkers often hold their tongue. But now the only sound was Martina Navratilova muttering to herself. 'Come on, come on,' she said, as in the third set the balance of power went to and fro.

In the stands, Mike Estep, Martina's coach since 1983, screwed up his round face as she prepared to stave off a match point; young Graf had her fingers on the hem of the US championship. When Martina took the point, Estep, in a gesture of relief, covered his face with his hand.

She was forced to save three match points before she triumphed on her own third match point. But in that third-set tie-break, even the spectators were emotionally exhausted. Navratilova had had to call on all of the muscle and concentration and stamina and nerve that nature and strict training had given her – and all the technical skill. She had a range of shots and an ability to place them that showed up the powerhouses of men's tennis. At 10–8 she won the tie-break to win the match, 6–1, 6–7, 7–6. It had been exquisite tennis.

Relief etched itself into her face. Estep felt it too. But both of them felt apprehension that they knew would not go away. Steffi was there. She would always be there now, lurking. The stakes were high and ultimately the ending was bound to be tragic. Meanwhile, Martina opted for comic relief.

'Can I have some water please before I die?' an exhausted Martina Navratilova said after the hundredth Open semi-final.

Victorious, the woman who had been fielding questions about retiring for years now quipped: 'If Steffi keeps playing this well, I'll have to quit.'

After the match, Estep also gave some interviews. 'Martina is totally motivated,' he said, with a pleasant grin on that moon face. 'When she came to me in 1983 and said she wanted to become the best player she could be, she was already number one.' Her astute obsessive pounding of tennis balls had affected more than just Navratilova's own tennis: '*She* went to work,' he stressed, 'and all of a sudden she had upped the ante. The stakes were changed, so was the game.' Indeed, at top level, the women's game was, arguably, now more interesting than the men's. (Few cared to make the argument, however.) The women's game at its best relied more on strategy than strength. Strength was to an excellent serve-and-volley player less necessary than stamina; finesse was even more valuable. Increasingly the men's game was a young man's game – bam bam bam – hard unreturnable shots, not deftly placed ones. Too quick to be satisfying.

The crowd at Flushing Meadow had patriotically applauded the winner, the Czechomerican, Navratilova. In the days when America was called the melting pot and the Statue of Liberty waved welcome to the tired, toiling and poor, quite a number of ethnicities appeared, Czech-Americans among them. But the Czechomerican, characterized by several abodes in several states of the union, a big income and expensive tennis rackets which she (or he – let's not forget Ivan Lendl) has received by the gross and gratis, is a brand new, much welcomed, American ethnicity.

After defecting from Czechoslovakia, Martina Navratilova had been granted refugee status in the United States and became an American citizen six years later on 21 July 1981. On the day of her 1986 semi-final victory at the hundredth Open, she was annoyed when the ladies and gentlemen of the press called her Czech, and she said so: 'Come on, I'm an American. You can't go on where we were born. If you do that McEnroe would be German.' John McEnroe was born in Wiesbaden. He was quintessentially American, and at that moment, Boris Becker's moment, he wasn't a good enough player to be German.

There are cycles in tennis history, eras, in which players from one nation tend to dominate. Just now in women's tennis, it was Czechoslovakia. The compact Hana Mandlikova, who had two houses in the US and who would later get a new legal base in Australia, had faced down the Czech-American, Martina Navratilova, in the 1985 US Open final. Now the 1986 final of the Centennial US Open pitted Martina Navratilova against the tall, grasshopper-thin, third Czech, six-foot two-inch Helena Sukova. Two years earlier, at the Australian Open, Sukova, a moderately talented, workmanlike player, had ended Martina's great 74-match winning streak, the longest one in women's tennis. Her mother Vera, remember, had been the Czech national coach when Martina defected; and there were those who thought that when she played Martina, Helena Sukova had a lot to prove. 'There is a lot of baggage happening when I play her,' Martina says. 'That's another tricky one. I'll have to keep playing the ball and not get into the past, because it's easy to get overwhelmed by it.'

Now Sukova, whose mother had taught both of them some of what they knew, sliced, dinked, lobbed and perpetrated a particularly wristy topspin to the best of her ability, but Martina prevailed to win her third US Open 6–3, 6–2.

With Hana and Helena up there with Martina, it was evident that the Czech era had arrived in tennis. Yet Graf, the young West German, was already there, waiting, as she had just demonstrated at the semi-final of the Open, not entirely in the wings.

What had become of the American challenge? A glum Chris Evert Lloyd, of whom this question was often asked, had a defensive answer ready: 'We still have a lot of good American players, especially in the women. We have Stephanie Rehe and Mary Joe Fernandez . . .'

Who? Teenagers, but by no means prodigies; players with too few strokes to their games. Chris clones. When she was still Miss Evert, Chris swapped double-fisted backhanders with fourteen-year-old Tracy Austin, who had pig-tails and braces on her teeth. Tracy had done damage to Martina on occasion. Now, it was Mary Joe Fernandez, who had also appeared on the scene at fourteen, with the same braces and backhand. Watching her play Chris Evert was like watching the same player at each end of the court. 'She's my idol,' Mary Joe said of Chris. 'My game is pretty much modelled on hers.'

At thirty-one Chris Evert Lloyd had found her harder work than Tracy had been. 'She's physically stronger than Tracy was when she was fourteen. And in ten years time you'll be seeing even stronger fourteen-year-olds.' That was surely because of diet and fitness techniques, not muscle-building drugs.

When Chrissie began to dominate in the 1970s, coaches began to tell their girls to hug the baseline. The failure of a tennis generation of Americans was partly because at the very time when Martina was raising the athletic stakes, their game had been modelled on Chrissie's limited example. Thus do role models function, for good and evil.

When Billie Jean King was pre-eminent, every girl's game, if at all possible, was serve and volley. Indeed, that had been the American way of tennis since the late 1930s, when that other talented Californian Alice Marble was wowing Wimbledon. Marble helped Billie in her early days, just as she had helped Haynie help Martina. Martina had forced Chris to raise her game and her fitness to a new level, and if we were now in an era of boring baseliners, they were baseliners with iron thighs.

Most tennis players will tell you they are entertainers – even Olympic athletes tell you that these days – supposedly that's why they merit all that money. It is a debased notion of sport. The gladiator keeping the Roman crowd's mind off the dire state of the Republic; a circus of athletes instead of caged lions. You know those clichés.

Martina, the highest prize-money winner, and she had to be with all those endorsements down the drain, was as interested in money as the rest of them – sport is the apogee of greed. But her pride was in her craft, in her game.

The Centennial Open, Martina Navratilova's fourteenth grand slam singles title, yielded a winner's prize of $210,000 (£140,000). That was precisely the same pay as Ivan Lendl, the winner of the men's title, received for potentially more work – in women's tennis you could win in two straight sets, men had to win a minimum of three. It was a 12 per cent increase over the previous year. Martina's purses that year would be 1.4 million dollars. She was at the top of the Money List. Eight years later, with twenty million dollars, she would still be top when she retired. Martina was lucky in her era. Billie Jean King had by the end of her tennis career pulled in only two million dollars. But by 1986 Martina, who as a player had ranked number one in the world alternately with Chris since 1978 (except for the few months of Tracy Austin in 1980), was not really after money any more. It was mainly history, those tiny notations in the record books, that she was after now. But life was already wonderful: 'This is the third time I have won Wimbledon and the US Open in the same year,' said Martina. 'This in addition to my return to Prague in the Federation Cup has really made this a summer to remember for me.'

At the Wimbledon final of 1987, where the going was always going to be tough, Martina took no chances. All season, Steffi Graf had been a giant killer – she had behind her a string of over forty victories, among them her first grand slam win, at the French Open, where Martina double-faulted on the last point to lose the final 6–4, 4–6, 8–6. In the weeks before Wimbledon, Martina, on a losing streak, even switched to

Graf's brand of racket. Martina said she could hit the ball harder with it. To appease her irate sponsors, she stencilled their monogram on the other manufacturer's racket. Martina's supporters shook their heads gloomily. You can only win when you play your own game. How could she win playing with Graf's racket? 'Nothing is worse,' Martina would say, 'than when people say you're washed up.' They had been saying it all season. But Wimbledon would be Martina's first meeting with Steffi Graf on grass, and grass *was* Martina Navratilova's surface, Wimbledon her home. Her serve was still efficient; her will on occasion mighty. But many thought she now lacked the confidence to win against Steffi Graf. 'Though there was pressure because I hadn't won anything,' Martina recalls, 'I think it also took some pressure off, because I wasn't expected to win.' Renee Richards, recalled to the team, offered Martina a very simple strategy: serve to the backhand only.

The American boxer Sugar Ray Leonard, who was friendly with Judy and Martina, had given Martina a miniature tennis racket for luck. She stuffed it into her sock and went out on to the court. She served the first ball of the Wimbledon final to the eighteen-year-old Steffi Graf. Graf won the point.

Martina's supporters in the crowd caught their breath. This was the year Chris Evert would be relegated to the grand slam semi-finals; was it also the end for Martina? No. Wimbledon again inspired Martina. After thirty-nine minutes, she won the first set. Another half an hour, and it was over, Martina victorious, 7–5, 6–3. 'I never lost my serve in that match.' And the only time the younger player had led on points was on that first one.

On that calm, windless day Martina Navratilova and the crowd felt tremendous excitement as she equalled Helen Wills Moody's fifty-year-old record of eight singles titles. She one-upped Suzanne Lenglen's sixty-year-old record of five *consecutive* titles. She also became the first woman to match William Renshaw's men's record of six consecutive titles. Billie Jean King had won six times, but not consecutively.

'How many more Wimbledons do you want?' Steffi asked as they awaited the Duchess of Kent's presentation of the trophies.

'Nine is my lucky number,' Martina answered. That would give her the outright singles record. 'Once I got to eight, it was kind of silly not to go after it,' Martina says.

At the US Open, once again she faced Steffi in the final. The powerful, swift swords of Steffi's serve and forehand at first seemed indomitable. The turning point of the match came during the first-set tie-breaker, when at 3–3 Steffi nervously missed two backhands. Martina triumphed again, 7–6 (7–4), 6–1, winning the Open for the fourth time. Martina won the doubles with Pam Shriver and the mixed doubles with Arantxa Sanchez Vicario's older brother Emilio Sanchez. Not since Margaret Court had accomplished it in 1970 had any woman won the US Open triple crown.

The following year, though, Steffi would win 5–7, 6–2, 6–1 at Wimbledon – and cut out Martina's heart. Even before that, the computer broke it. Towards the end of the 1987 season, it treacherously moved Steffi Graf ahead of Martina to the number one position in the world rankings.

Martina disputed the new ranking. 'If you win Wimbledon and the Open, you've won the biggest tournaments of the year,' Martina said. 'I think that makes you number one no matter what the computer says.' Many agreed with her; but the computer's verdict stood.

Although Martina had been a finalist in all the major tournaments, she had won only four of the twelve events she entered. For the first time in half a dozen years, Martina earned less than a million dollars in prize money. There could be little pleasure in getting $932,102 in a year in which young Steffi garnered $1,063,785.

In 1988, no one could dispute Steffi's pre-eminence. She won all four grand slam events to achieve that rarity, the Grand Slam. Hers was the purist's version, all four in the same calendar year, which Martina had never managed. Steffi Graf would hold on to the number one world ranking for a record 186 consecutive weeks until March of 1991, when the Florida-based Yugoslav Monica Seles took over for a few months. Martina had been world number one at season's end from 1982 to 1986, but had held the ranking for only 156 consecutive weeks – from June 1982 to June 1985. After Steffi reached the top of the rankings, Martina would never again be world number one.

In 1988, she reached the final of only one grand slam tournament, Wimbledon, losing to Steffi and again ending the season as world number two. An era seemed to be ending in tennis. Chris Evert was on the brink of retirement. Chris won at their seventy-seventh meeting, but Martina won their last three matches, concluding the greatest rivalry in tennis with a 6–2, 6–2 victory in Chicago. Their final match record was 43–37 in Martina's favour.

The previous generation had lived to defeat Navratilova; the new ones already thought of Graf. Only Arantxa Sanchez Vicario could tell you when she first met Martina, in Florida in 1987, and that was solely because of something Martina said: 'I lost but Martina told me I would be a great champion some day.'

In 1989, as Steffi continued her domination, Martina was visibly fading. Wasn't this the end of the road for Martina? Wasn't it time to quit? Why did Martina, whose joy in the game had been extinguished, keep banging her head against Steffi's racket? It was not until her loss to Gabriela Sabatini in the semi-final at Amelia Island, in April 1989, that a despairing Martina, in need of renewal, telephoned Billie Jean King and said, 'Help.'

Billie agreed to come to her assistance on one condition. 'I want you to take full responsibility; it's gonna be your choice, your deal.'

Impulsively, Martina said, 'I'll do it, let's go.'

But were they going to mend her game, Billie wanted to know, or more or less start over? 'We'll work with what you have if that's what you want' – or they would dissect her technique. 'This is your choice, it's your journey.'

Realizing that nothing less would work, Martina chose the harder option. They changed her volleys, they were working on her serve. Billie brought in other people. 'I'm a big believer in bringing other people in including a lot of different theories.' They still weren't happy with her serve.

Martina would listen to everything, try it, and then choose what she thought would work for her. Some of it did; some of it didn't. With so many changes to her game, few of them yet felt natural. Martina's head was abuzz with technique; visions of the new strokes dancing like sugarplum fairies in her head. A ninth victory would be Christmas. But was it possible? Graf seemed invincible.

Then came an unexpected gift from seventeen-year-old Sanchez Vicario. Her triumph over Steffi Graf at the French Open denied Steffi a second Grand Slam and prevented her from equalling Martina's 1983–84 feat of winning six consecutive grand slams, which many regard as a greater achievement than the Grand Slam.

Wimbledon was looming. Billie said to Martina, 'You might win this year, but don't count on it.'

Unwanted distractions were kept to a minimum. Now it was Judy who would show the journalists through their houses. Nothing was hidden in this their life, even though these days Martina barely had a spare moment. One of the first rooms on the Fort Worth house tour was the master bedroom. The room was more suggestive of triumph than bliss. It was where Martina's trophies were now kept. Judy had assembled everything.

'I made it my quest to get these things.' She showed off the pride of trophies, the silver cups and bowls, the framed letter from Katharine Hepburn – the solid evidence of a lifetime of celebrity. 'I found them where Martina had left them: in people's attics, in storage, with agents, with strangers.' All eight of the little salad-sized chased-silver plates that the winner of Wimbledon gets to keep – the big platter goes back to the tournament – were there, lined up together on a shelf. But two of the US Open trophies were missing. Judy was hunting for them still.

At Wimbledon 1989, Martina reached the finals where she lost to Steffi 6–2, 6–7, 6–1. They had nearly done it; but nearly doesn't count. Billie's sympathy was, as ever, highly pragmatic. 'You have three hundred sixty-five more days to prepare.'

The rest of the world decided it was too late. She was finished in the competitive age of Graf and Seles. With the advent of Arantxa Sanchez Vicario and all the others, not even Martina Navratilova could rise yet again from the dead. But Martina, now thirty-three, still wanted what everyone thought impossible for someone of her age in that tennis climate. She wanted to win a ninth Wimbledon. 'Am I insatiable? Yes,' said Martina. 'Wimbledon is like a drug.'

Martina and Judy took time off from tennis in April 1990 to return to Czechoslovakia, which was having its first political spring since 1968. They both wept when they visited the gravesite of Martina's grandmother. Martina took away a stone from the ground over which her grandmother's ashes had been spread.

Prague is a small city, and Ian Dusek, the young man who was not yet the women's coach at Stvanice tennis centre, pulled his jacket collar up around his throat against the breeze that was coming off the river and walked over to Wenceslaus Square to a meeting that had been called by the radical poet and playwright Vaclav Havel. In the Velvet Revolution of November 1989 the Communists had been thrown out, but some people were still a little nervous that it might all fizzle. The crowd of 200,000 was astonished to see Martina, whose visit had not been announced. She and Judy had run into Havel at a restaurant, and he had invited her to speak to the populace from the famous platform. Along with Havel himself who would inspire the transition from communism and become the country's leader in the first free election, Martina spoke movingly of freedom. Ian Dusek was not the only young man who wept.

To Martina, looking out over that huge, responsive crowd, it must have been a heady feeling to realize she could be a political force.

In 1990, Billie continued as her coach-motivator. It was Craig who would call her to arrange the jolts. Working with Martina every day, he knew he needed someone to come in periodically, cast a cool eye, but generate enthusiastic heat. By now they had established the routine which would endure until Martina's retirement. Billie worked with her a crucial week here, a crucial week there, for eight to twelve weeks of the year. 'I usually go to Aspen for Christmas and stay an extra week. That's when she starts,' Billie Jean King explains. 'Craig comes up to Aspen. One year I was by myself because he couldn't come, he was buying a house.' Martina and Judy's Colorado estate outside Aspen more than rivalled Flordon, where Martina had lived with Rita Mae. Billie also delivered jolts in Chicago where she lived and Martina liked to play, at Hillton Head, and at Eastbourne in England prior to Wimbledon. Going into Wimbledon 1990, Martina would try to play more matches. In the words of the old Haynie wisdom, she would get match tough. By now, too, all that information had stopped whirring around inside Martina's head. The technical improvements to her game had been properly absorbed.

There is no divine right in tennis, but the greatest champions, like ancient monarchs, have a close connection with magic and mythology. Phoenix-like, Martina's heart regrew in her body. She had been healed of burn-out, refound her love of tennis, and now her power seemed to be rekindled. But was life really mythic? After three years without a grand slam victory, could a 33-year-old with wonky knees make the miracle of a ninth Wimbledon really happen? When Team Navratilova arrived at Wimbledon in 1990 they found that the media had largely written Martina off.

'They didn't think she had a chance,' recalls Billie. 'And I just said, you guys don't get it.'

Every expectation was overturned at that Wimbledon; not just the media's. It was Zina Garrison, not Steffi, whom Martina had to face in the final. Steffi Graf's allergies, the fallout from a sex scandal involving her father, and a Garrison playing exceptionally well, combined to defeat Steffi in the semi.

Martina was almost disappointed. 'I was so ready for Steffi,' she said. She had lost to Zina only once in twenty-seven matches. All the bets were on Martina. 'The only question in my mind,' she said, 'was if my knees were going to hold up.'

On the night before the final, Zina Garrison, who didn't have a clothing contract largely because she was African-American – the big corporations preferred snub-nosed blondes – signed a six-figure deal with Reebok. Until then, Garrison had been wearing Martina's signature clothing line – the one Judy and Martina had started because Martina too failed to appeal to the big corporations. An American television station flew Althea Gibson, the only black woman ever to win Wimbledon, over to provide moral support. Gibson's two titles had been more than thirty years earlier.

In the TV commentary box, sitting beside NBC's Bud Collins, was Chris Evert in her new part-time job as anchor. 'I just know what it means to both of these players, they're friends of mine,' Chris told the audience, 'and I saw them in the locker room earlier. They're both nervous but in different ways. Martina is just so excited about playing, but she's a wreck. I mean she's running around the locker room. I have never seen her this nervous.' Zina, on the other hand, was hiding her nerves under a mask of apparent composure.

On court, Martina let the well-tuned machine that was her body do its precision work. As Garrison mishit her final backhand, Martina raised her arms, and sank to her sore knees, in what looked like a silent prayer of thanksgiving. She had won 6–4, 6–1. Chris in the commentary box was suddenly mute. 'I couldn't say a word, I got caught up in the emotions of it. She was the greatest grass-court player that Wimbledon had ever seen.'

No longer was Martina right up there with the great Helen Wills Moody. Moody's record, set eighteen years before Martina was born, held for fifty-two years. Now Martina had surpassed it. Martina's ninth victory, like the finale of Beethoven's ninth symphony, was to her great jubilation erupting from sorrow.

To share the exquisite, the joyous moment, just as Pat Cash did when he won, Martina climbed up to her friends in the stands. She hugged Craig and kissed him, then Billie, then Judy. It was that last embrace that caused the comment. 'I had no idea I was going to do that,' Martina says. 'I wasn't making a statement other than this is the person that I love.'

At the press conference it was pointed out that the one-sided Wimbledon final had been far from the best ever. 'It was my match to win and I wasn't afraid of it,' said Martina, adding memorably, 'they don't put an asterisk next to your name denoting that you didn't play well.'

On the walk home from Wimbledon to the house they always rented, Martina and Judy, accompanied by security guards, were followed by fans and photographers. Judy remembers the joy of the moment as they arrived at the gate where their friends were waiting. 'Martina was showered with flowers and champagne.' With a platoon of tennis greats and other friends, they ate and ate in one of London's Chinese restaurants that night. Chris Evert was there, so were Billie Jean King, Craig Kardon, Rosie Casals, the former tennis prodigy Andrea Jaeger, Julie Anthony, who owned the Aspen Club where Martina had filmed her exercise video, and Gigi Fernandez, a former doubles partner and now an Aspen neighbour. The celebratory meal went on for four hours.

In Chicago, in 1992, in the midst of a painful and very public 'divorce' from Judy, Martina defeated the young Czech serve and volleyer Jana Novotna to break Chris Evert's all-time tournament win record of 157. Now Martina had won 158.

'That was the best she ever played me,' Jana Novotna, another heiress apparent, would say of that Chicago match years later, 'but I don't know how well she was capable of playing, I never played her in her prime.'

Judy Nelson's lawyer had filed suit at the worst possible time, just before Wimbledon 1991. Before handing Martina the official notification, the process server asked for an autograph. Angrily, Martina asked for the autograph back.

The 'divorce' was of the worst sort, hostile and messy. Much of it was televised. According to the 'nonmarital cohabitation' agreement the two women had signed, Judy was claiming half of what Martina had earned during their years together.

'For seven years I have supported and assisted Martina, sacrificing many of my own personal goals in the process,' said Judy, who was forty-five. 'She has left me and pursued another relationship, and left my life in disarray.'

'I not only took care of Judy,' Martina countered, citing salaries and chapter and verse, 'but of course her family, provided help with her parents and her kids and their friends — flying people all over the place.' In addition to luxury on the tennis circuit, their houses in Fort Worth and Aspen, the villa on Antigua, and the apartment at Trump Plaza in New York, only the year before, they had begun building a 7000-square-foot dream house on a hundred acres near Aspen.

Martina, it was suggested, had sought renewal again in another woman. 'I did not leave Judy for a younger woman or anyone else,' she said. 'We just parted.' Cindy Nelson, the former ski champion, now a ski instructor, was mentioned, and denied that they were anything more than friends. Many people in Colorado believe this to be true.

It was during the last months of 1988 that Judy had first suspected that Martina was involved with a ski instructor. Although Judy was jealous, especially when Martina gave her friend a diamond necklace for Christmas, she felt that she and Martina had talked through the problem. In 1989 Martina and

Judy moved from Fort Worth to Aspen. Judy's sons and her parents, who had always been in close proximity, stayed in Texas; now the couple were more on their own.

Things began to deteriorate. The clothing business which Judy and Martina had started when Martina lacked endorsements had never been the success they wanted; but even as one dream failed to materialize fully, the couple was creating another, the ranch which was their dream house, where after they separated Martina would live. There was the tension of Martina's knee operation in December 1990; it was a success. That Christmas, 1990, her parents and sister came to visit in Colorado, but on New Year's Eve Judy was rushed to hospital with a spastic colon. When Judy returned from hospital Martina was out skiing. There were painful discussions.

The crunch came on 3 February 1991, the night they returned from Tokyo, the last tournament Judy would attend with Martina, and where Martina had lost in the three-set final to Gabriela Sabatini. That night, discovering for sure that Martina was seriously involved with another woman, Judy demanded Martina leave the house.

'Where will I go?' Martina said. 'It's the middle of the night. Can I just sleep in another room?'

'No, you have to leave. You can go up to the ranch.' Their ranch was not far. 'You can't stay here with me when you feel that you are in love with someone else,' Judy said. As she wanted Martina, this was perhaps the stupidest action of Judy's life. Judy admits that she had become bossy in the last years of their relationship. Now, not only did she throw out Martina, she insisted Martina first wake up Judy's parents who were visiting and explain why she was going. Soon they were all crying. Judy says she never dreamed that would be Martina's last night in their house. Both sons wrote letters asking Martina to come back. But their life together was over.

IMG tried unsuccessfully to negotiate a financial settlement. 'At this point, without her knowledge, all credit cards, car and health insurance, and access to checking and saving accounts had been stripped away,' Judy and her co-author say in *Love Match*. Judy maintains that although she was unaware of it at first, the accounts had been frozen the day after Martina left, on Martina's instructions. She says she found out when one of her credit cards was refused.

In March, during a tense telephone conversation with Judy, Martina very reasonably asked, 'What is it that you want?'

'I want what was in the agreement,' Judy says she replied, a reference to the notorious nonmarital cohabitation agreement that had been signed in 1986. Why, why, why, didn't Judy say, 'I want you.' 'I told her a million times that I wanted her,' says Judy. Now, it was too late. Martina would never come back. She had cut, turning her back on Judy just as she had on Czechoslovakia.

As the prospect of a tenth Wimbledon title disappeared in the ill wind, Martina said, 'A year ago I didn't know if I would get the record at Wimbledon because my body was so sore. But at least I thought I knew where I was going to live and who I was going to live with once my career did end. Now I don't know anything, except that all I can do is play the best tennis I can.'

Against Judy's wishes, the court proceedings were televised. Judy says she had to file suit to have money to live. Rita Mae Brown counselled both parties, and finally it was settled out of court, costing Martina millions in legal fees anyway. 'It is an ugly end to what, by all accounts, has been the happiest of alternative marriages,' bemoaned *People* magazine.

Many thought Judy had acted out of spite. 'No,' Martina told *The Advocate* in 1993. 'She really truly believes she deserves half that money. She somehow convinced herself of that.' Martina, however, had neither forgiven nor forgotten. 'All I know is if I had done what she had done, I couldn't look myself in the mirror.'

The amount of the settlement Judy received was never made public, 'and it never will be,' says Judy. The house alone was worth in the region of a million dollars. But Judy maintains that the settlement did not make her rich. 'I will tell you this,' she says. 'If it was like people think or thought, I would be on some island drinking pina coladas now. I pay for half of my sons' education. I'm a working single mother just like anybody else.' When I asked her in September 1994 if she would still go back, Judy said, 'No. Six months ago I finally came to that. That was a very important eight years of my life but this part of my life is about who I am. I'm not the woman behind the woman any more, I'm my own person.' Both Martina and Judy saw therapists in the aftermath of their parting.

Judy Nelson, the woman scorned at forty-five, soon found solace, and even began a relationship with Rita Mae. They remain friends. Despite Judy's new alliances, after the lawsuit was settled she implied years later on television that she was still in love with Martina.

Until the spring of 1994 Judy would have gone back to Martina, but then she fell in love. With a woman. Judy lectures on marriage and law and does some television commentary on the American gay cable channel. 'Not everybody loves what I'm doing,' she says. 'Not even the gay community accepts me totally.' Why? 'Because I hurt their hero.'

Yes. And the hero hurt her.

~ 11 ~

Sexual Politics

With her bare feet tucked under her on the huge sofa and her tiny fox terrier KD nestling in her lap, Martina gazed out at the future. The rented American condominium apartment which faced the beach had an impressive view. The future was equally beautiful. 'Because of tennis,' she said truthfully, 'I have the opportunity to do anything. I'm sure I'll be an activist either for the environment or for gay rights or maybe for both.'

She was known already as an advocate of both issues. In April 1993 she had said to Billie, 'I'm going on this march in two weeks.'

'What?'

'In Washington.'

'I haven't heard of it.'

'You're kidding?'

'No. Why didn't you call me [earlier], I would have gone. That's human rights.'

Martina and at least half a million other people strode past the White House, down Pennsylvania Avenue, waving rainbow flags, symbols of gay liberation. There were so many people marching in the sun in that trailing political procession that it took six hours to reach the Mall. Many speakers of both sexual orientations linked the event in spirit and ambition to the historic 1963 Civil Rights March on Washington where Martin Luther King announced, 'I have a dream.'

Martin Luther King's heir as civil rights leader, Jesse L. Jackson said, 'No more homophobia. Let's respect people, protect people.'

Martina said, 'What our movement for equality needs most is for us to come out of the closet. Let's come out and dispel all the rumours. Let's come out and set everybody straight, so to speak.'

Congressman Barney Frank, one of the two openly gay members of the House of Representatives, warned that gay people 'would no longer submit to unequal treatment' and said that the religious groups that were opposing them were using religion 'as a stick with which to beat other people'.

The march by gays was the culmination of a week of ceremonies and protests to secure more funding for AIDS care and research, to win passage of legislation that would ban discrimination, and to affirm their lives.

The *Washington Post* went into the VIP tent near the Washington Monument and asked the 'big-name gay people and supporters' to rattle off postcards they might have sent from the march. 'Dear Jesus Christ,' said the twentieth-century icon and tennis star, 'I would love to hear what you would say if you were here today. Love, Martina.'

Jesus was very central to all this. The American Christian Right was not only damning homosexuality from the pulpit, as usual, it was also in the midst of a major legislative offensive. On election day, November 1992, in Martina's adopted home state of Colorado, it had come to the crunch. At the same time that they voted for the President, a 53 per cent majority of Colorado voters approved Amendment 2, which prohibits any new laws to protect lesbians and gay men from discrimination on the grounds of their sexuality. Amendment 2, also retroactive, overturned the existing anti-discrimination laws in the cities of Aspen, Boulder and Denver. 'Many people have said the wording was so confusing they did not know that their vote meant it was all right to discriminate,' wrote Martina, who had asked her friends and neighbours, in a guest column for a national newspaper. Other polls also suggested some voters didn't know. But now it was law.

Passionately, Martina spoke out against it. 'I realize what amendment two means to my civil rights or what this kind of measure can mean to African-Americans, disabled people, or any minority who could lose their rights too if a couple of words were changed.' The passage of Amendment 2 led to calls for a boycott of Colorado businesses. And many of the Hollywood beautiful people who usually skiied in Colorado shunned it that year. Martina vowed to leave Colorado if Amendment 2 was not overturned. 'I will not live in a state that does not recognize me as an equal citizen.'

But first she would stay to fight.

'The propaganda is that gay people are asking for special rights. We are not,' she told *Ladies' Home Journal*. 'We are asking for equality, for the same rights that everyone else has under the Constitution, the right not to be dismissed from a job or to be denied housing simply because of who we are.' Proponents of the law wanted to be able to dismiss gay teachers, firemen, social workers, and the like.

The organization that had originated the measure wanted to use it as a model for similar laws in other states. 'It's scary. What are they doing in people's bedrooms? Why is this their concern?' Sexual orientation 'is a very private part of our lives that you should be able to be private about – but you should not have to lie about'.

'Gays and lesbians are not different from other people. My sexual orientation has nothing to do with my ability to be a good citizen, or the role model people say I am,' Martina said. 'There are gays in all walks of life – doctors, lawyers, teachers, entertainers, construction workers, football players (gasp!) and, yes, the military. But the gay part is the private self. It only affects the individual and his or her partner. The public self –

154

the doctor or athlete – is the essential portion on which to question the person's performance. In other words, are they doing their job? That's what matters.'

The advocates of Amendment 2 and its clones were saying, she believed, that gay teachers would teach their students to be gay. 'Gay people can't be turned straight; the reverse is true, too. And the myth that we're this way by choice is ridiculous. Who would want to be gay and be ostracized and prejudiced against for most of their lives? Nobody wants that. It's not a choice.'

This argument may be fallacious. Some segments of the gay rights movement were advocating it to counteract the religious right's charge that homosexuals were immoral. How could you be immoral, if God made you that way? Others, however, regarded this as a dangerous argument. If God had made a developmental 'mistake', genetic scientists of the next generation would be set loose on foetuses to remedy it. Then what would happen to the literary genius of a Proust, the mathematical genius of an Alan Turing, the sporting prowess of a Navratilova or a Maria Bueno, the musical finesse of a Benjamin Britten?

The researcher Simon LeVay who advocates the nature not nurture view, that gays were born that way, is, as it happens, gay. Martina's argument is derived from Simon LeVay's theories. Actual data on the origin of homosexuality are inconclusive. LeVay admits that his views come as much from his politics as his science. He has documented a genetic basis for homosexuality only in about 50 per cent of his test cases, and all of his studies were on the brains of men who had died of AIDS. There is no way of knowing if the anomalies were caused by disease or by sexual orientation.

Martina lent her name to the American Civil Liberties Union lawsuit against Amendment 2, and in late 1994 the Colorado Supreme Court ruled that the bigoted amendment was unconstitutional. The case will probably continue to the Supreme Court. 'I left one totalitarian state,' Martina told a Colorado crowd during the campaign to overturn the law. If necessary, she would leave another.

Motherhood, a matter of emotion, was also in her case a political matter. There were those who thought Martina was not the best mother material on two counts. One she was lesbian; two, she was more used to being coddled than coddling.

But I think there is no reason Martina would not be a fine mother. Like most lesbians, she is the product of heterosexual parents. In fact she comes from that rarity, a fairly happy, fairly nondysfunctional family; her own upbringing taught her the importance of nurturing; Martina had Babicka and the other grandmother, her mother and her devoted stepfather. She knows, the way one knows best, from the gut, from childhood experience, how much attention children crave and need. She knows what it feels like to be on the receiving end of that attention and love. Too few prospective parents realize that raising children is exceedingly labour intensive. Martina's own childhood taught her the difference, too, between doting on her dog KD or her many other pets and raising a human child. As for father figures, if one needs them, Martina has extremely good relationships with a number of men. She has had the same male sports agent for the better part of fifteen years. 'I'm sure I'll adopt a kid or two – give somebody a good life, hopefully,' she says. 'The only question is whether I'll have one of my own as well, which I probably will. There are some people who feel gay couples should not be able to adopt children. What amazes me is that these people think they have the right to decide what rights other people may or may not have.'

— 12 —

Countdown

Twelve days before Christmas, 1993, London learned that Martina was sharing a flat near Sloane Square with a new companion. Eagle-nosed and Slavonic looking, Danda Jaroljmek had fashionably streaked, crinkly, brown and blonde, chin-length hair. Despite the unusual name, Danda was to all appearances British, with an accent that was fairly upper class.

Five years younger than Martina, Danda, who was studying sculpture and had worked for the designer Galliano, lived in an expensive bit of town, but she was so ordinary that her address and phone number were in the telephone directory.

Sloane Square is a part of London Martina knows well. More than a dozen years ago she rented a flat there during Wimbledon with Rita Mae. When the tabloids found out they came knocking. One who was certainly no gentleman had bribed a maid to get in. Martina and Danda were soon encountering the same prying inquisitors. None the less, they would survive the six months to Wimbledon.

Danda's interest in tennis is somewhat limited, or at least, that is my impression after sitting behind her at one of Martina's doubles matches at the French Open. Danda chatted about skiing to an acquaintance non-stop. Midway through the match, a friend sitting a dozen feet away called to her to come over. 'But you can see much better from here,' Danda said reasonably.

157

'I didn't come here to see the match, I came here to talk to you,' said the friend whose seat was separated from the VIP enclosure by a rail. Obligingly, Danda changed her seat.

Fifteen days before Christmas, according to London's premier gossip columnist Nigel Dempster, Martina had a tennis match with Diana, the Princess of Wales, at the Harbour Club. 'We played tennis in London in November,' Martina says. 'So that was the first time I'd gotten to know her, really. We had a blast.' At the time, Martina was playing tennis there just about daily. Danda went too. Prince Charles's younger brother Edward was also a regular.

Nigel Dempster broke the Danda story three days after it became widely known that Diana had played tennis with Martina. It is far-fetched even to contemplate the possibility that the Palace had cooperated in establishing the fact of Danda's existence, but it did dispel any uncomfortable notions that the princess might be interested in anything more than Martina's tennis. Every time Martina spoke to a woman, there were people who made assumptions. Diana had been an early visitor to AIDS sufferers, and sat through the vigil of a dying friend. Many admired her compassion and courage, but few of these admirers were functionaries at Buckingham Palace.

During Christmas itself came another Martina revelation, this time on television. The singer Melissa Etheridge, a friend of Martina's and about whom there had also been speculation, was hosting a gay alternative Christmas show. It was as light-weight and as sentimental as all the other Christmas shows, with the guest-star cameo appearances billed as holiday visits by and to friends. The camera took us to Martina's house in Colorado, where she invited us into her living room and wished us a very merry Christmas. Neither Danda nor Billie Jean King seemed to be present, but looking out of the big picture window you could see plenty of snow.

Martina began the 1994 tennis season full of hope, but Billie Jean King was worried. Martina was taking too much time off. 'I felt like she was taking too big a hiatus. She likes to take a long break – it's not just a holiday because she works out. Like after Chicago she likes six weeks. I keep telling Craig, and we keep telling her, he agrees, it's just too long, you need to be playing matches. Especially when you're older, you have to play matches. You'll have more bad matches, more flat days when you're older, but when you get to Wimbledon you'll have the peak that you want.' The complication is that the older you are the more tired you get too; it is not easy to get the balance right between being sluggish from too little activity or tired from too much.

Martina announced that 1994 would be her last season of singles. She was still writing down her goals every year – remember it had started as a list of her faults. Now it was a list of priorities. 'Put 'em down and we'll help you, we'll support you any way we can,' said Billie.

Wimbledon was top of Martina's list. The fast grass courts of Wimbledon demand legs, which was what Martina didn't have any more. She was two paces slower across court than in her prime.

'OK,' said Billie, 'I think you need to play a lot of clay and you need to play a lot of matches, and it doesn't matter if you have a lot of losses. It's gonna help you so you can run when you need to.' Martina was in agreement.

In 1992 she had won four tournaments, including her sentimental favourite Chicago, and had reached the Wimbledon semi-final where she lost to Monica Seles, 6–2, 6–7, 6–4. In 1993 she won five, among them Eastbourne. At Wimbledon she lost for the first time to Jana Novotna 6–4, 6–4 in the semi, ending the season ranked third.

The 1994 season started well. In February Martina fell honourably to Steffi in the Tokyo final. Later that month, Martina defeated the French player Julie Halard in straight sets to win the little Paris indoor, the Open Gaz de France. It was Martina's 167th career singles title, which put her ten up on the world. Chris Evert, who had won 157 titles, ranked second.

But the American tune-up tournaments were sheer disaster.

In Chicago, she lost her second match. Houston, Texas turned out to be an even more unpleasant shock. On one level, to Martina, Texas would probably always be a reminder of Judy, and therefore synonymous with ultimate disaster. But Martina was fairly good at keeping her heart and her racket in separate compartments. And Texas had a lot of other memories for Martina too. Now, bidding for her seventh title at the 1994 Virginia Slims of Houston, she fell to an unknown in the second round, which, because she had a bye, was her opening match. The young Argentinian Bettina Fulco-Villella, ranked 231st in the world, was as horrified as Martina herself. In tears, she said, 'I wanted to say something to her, but nothing came out.'

The Argentinian's guilt, her identification with the hurt inflicted on Martina, boded ill for her future career – unless a sports psychologist was called in to rewire her moral imagination, or rather disconnect it. 'It's my biggest win,' the young Argentinian blurted. 'I still can't believe it.' Fulco was regarded as such a no-hoper she had been dropped from the 1994 WTA Media Guide.

There was some consolation: Martina and her new Dutch doubles partner Manon Bollegraf won their first title. Martina also fitted in a visit to the NASA Space Center. Hilton Head, South Carolina, a week later, was the second consecutive tournament in which Martina lost in her opening match, an alignment of the zodiac which hadn't occurred since 1974. For Martina's vanquisher, another Argentinian Ines Gorrochategui, it was her biggest win. Martina sloughed it off, 'It was a slugfest and she won in the end.' When a week after that, at Amelia Island in early April, Martina reached the semi, where she lost in straight sets to Arantxa Sanchez Vicario, the world number two, it was considered progress.

Billie had warned her not to worry about defeat. And she told the media she wasn't worrying, she was right on target: 'I just felt I wanted more matches going into Wimbledon because I felt last year I wasn't sharp because I hadn't played enough.' It was hard to look happy when you were losing. It didn't help either that the media persisted in asking her difficult questions about the nature of the new life that would begin at the end of her farewell tour.

'This is not a farewell tour. This is my last year on the circuit,' she insisted. The media were not alone in ignoring this distinction. Everyone, even her friend Pam Shriver, spoke of Martina's farewell tour. *Inside Women's Tennis*, the official WTA magazine, reported that 'Navratilova's Farewell Tour continued'.

Martina is fastidious about language, perhaps because she studied English and is therefore often more aware of nuances than its native speakers. Team Navratilova always consisted of a lot of people – coaches, nutritionists, physios, girlfriends, etc – but when the media started talking about her entourage, Martina made it known she preferred the word coterie.

Now, she spoke of a sense of finality which was accompanying her on this season. 'It is rough. I try not to think about it. When I do, I get misty-eyed. I know this is the last time, and it would probably have been easier on myself if I hadn't said, this is my last year. But it gets – I think because I played so many years, so many, it is that much more difficult to let go.'

If she was not to go out with a whimper, she needed to begin to make an impression on the season. A few days before it became public knowledge that Steffi Graf was withdrawing from the Italian Open, which began on the second of May, the WTA's London office said chattily that Martina might decide to play Rome. Whereupon, Steffi Graf dropped out. Martina, it was announced, was filling in.

The Foro Italico is a helluva place. Red clay surrounded by marble walkways. A regiment of marble statues standing guard on the gargantuan marble steps. A Rome reminiscent of Miami. Play began each day at 1 p.m. which left time for sightseeing. Martina's friend and neighbour Gigi Fernandez examined the Pantheon with her coach the psychologist Julie Anthony. With them was Gigi's doubles partner Natalia Zvereva. Gigi and Natalia were the world's top-ranked doubles team.

Conchita Martinez, who had beaten Martina here three times and was the defending champion, visited the Colosseum, where the ancient gladiators fought for the gift of their lives. Conchita's friend the blonde-haired Australian player Louise Pleming accompanied her. Martinez, the Junoesque, raven-haired, world number three, who had just turned twenty-two, partook liberally of the hazelnut gelato. Allegedly, the strawberry and coffee ones were Martina's favourites. Martina, still interested in architecture, ventured outside the city to the Emperor Hadrian's villa.

The group frequented a restaurant called Mario, three streets away from the Piazza de Espana. At home in Aspen Julie Anthony ran the Aspen club, where Martina and Gigi, who were once doubles partners, sometimes worked out together. They had the same trainer. They practised together too. You hear a lot about players avoiding each other and staying cocooned in their entourages. These were some of Martina's friends.

Each night, Conchita Martinez, whose serve had been clocked at 102 m.p.h. earlier in the season, visited the Trevi fountain and threw coins in the water. Her wish, no longer a secret, was to win the Italian Open.

First, she had to face Martina in the final. Clay was Conchita's best surface. It was Martina's worst. The Italian Open final would be classic, the outstanding serve-and-volley player on the way down, versus a young baseliner on the way up. There had been so many upsets in the tournament that Martina and Conchita each faced just one seeded opponent on their way to the final. 'Don't talk to me about lack of talent [in women's tennis],' Martina said. 'I'm ranked number four and I struggled to get to the semi-finals.' Yes, and she had been hard pressed there too. Martinez had also had her woes.

All this talk about the paucity of talent in women's tennis is empty. They have been saying the same thing since the golden age of Court and King.

The final itself was the sort you kick yourself over. Martina led 3–0 in the first set and held two set points on her serve, but lost the set anyway, 6–7. In the second set, at 4–all, Martina was broken at love, and Conchita then served out the match, Martina losing the set 4–6. Rome gave the runner-up a standing ovation that lasted three minutes. Everyone knows Italians are demonstrative. But this. Martina wept.

She was playing much better than she had in the States. Next on the agenda was the French Open, a grand slam tournament. It too is played on clay, which can be hard on the knees. Also playing on clay meant you weren't playing on grass, and Wimbledon was looming. Billie and Craig had wanted her to play a lot and play a lot of clay, though the Italian hadn't been on the original agenda. Now that it had been added, they were for changing gear and omitting the Open in Paris.

'Craig Kardon my coach and Billie Jean King didn't want me to come, but seeing this was my last year, I really wanted to play one last time. I have some pretty good memories here, and I wanted some better ones from this year.' And so it was against their better judgement that Martina kept her rendezvous in Paris.

Danda was at Stade Roland Garros wearing a lot of clothes for a summery day in May. The long dark-red dress, just shy of being burgundy, was of a coarse-grained, thick, cottony fabric. Fashionably shapeless, it hung like a caftan, hovering not much above the ankle. The hair highlighted, dark at the roots in the modern manner, crinkled to the shoulder.

It was eight years since Martina had played at Roland Garros. As she herself told one of the young players who asked the way to the WTA office, 'The only thing I recognize about the place is Centre Court.' She and Pam Shriver won the doubles here five times in a row. In 1982 and 1984, Martina won the singles. 'Two is not anything to sneeze at,' she said, but the two close finals that got away nagged her, one against Chris, the other against Steffi. 'If I had had a forehand down the line back then, I think I would have won both those matches. I could have won four [titles] which would have been a fantastic record.'

Practice at Court 16 was being watched from afar by about a dozen fans, some of whom had binoculars. Security guards at the steps down to the practice courts barred them from going any nearer. The press of course could cling to the sideboards of the courts if they wanted to. The class system is always clear-cut in sport; at any major championship in any major sport, colour-coded admission badges announce where you fit into the pecking order. Craig was hitting with Martina, and Billie Jean King was on court, advising. Each time Martina made a decent shot, Billie called out, 'Good,' and Gert chased the ball. Only recently had the German middle-aged fan attained the rank of ball girl. Martina, who was wearing the French Open souvenir shorts with the repeated tennis racket pattern, also had on a white T-shirt with the singer Melissa Etheridge on it. Throughout the practice Danda was chatting with a South African woman one saw a lot of on the circuit, a friend of Billie Jean King.

Craig hit a fairly sneaky shot to Martina's backhand. Running furiously, she just got it. 'Good,' said Billie. 'That's good, Martina.' Later she told me, 'I believe in the positive approach, at least three-quarters of the time.' Then Martina missed a shot. Then another. She was missing shots that in the past would have come easily.

Watching the practice, Tracey Bates, a knowledgeable English fan, felt worried. Last summer, Tracey had watched Martina play Miriam Oremans, a young Dutch player who looks a little like Billie, at the Eastbourne final. Martina won, but with difficulty. Oremans would be Martina's first-round opponent here. 'It will be a difficult match,' Tracey now decided. 'Martina could lose it.'

On the nearby courts, the other players were wearing shorts or tracksuit bottoms during practice, but Martina was the only one who played her matches in shorts. Most women felt compelled to wear little skirts that showed their knickers. Mary Pierce had found a more elegant solution: her tennis dresses over long, Lycra shorts provided flowing ease of movement, modesty and chic, and avoided chafed thighs. Martina's shorts were ugly and did nothing for her. Fashion, however, was the least of Martina's problems. Her timing was off.

The first-round match with Miriam Oremans on the first day of the tournament was played in gruelling sun and the clay was surprisingly fast. As the match progressed, Billie Jean King gnawed at her pinkie, and I found myself gnawing at mine. The great champion had never looked so merely human. Martina was missing shots, as she had in practice, because she couldn't get to them in time. The old champion quickly became the underdog. The French crowd was vocally picking her up and dusting her off after every attempt. And after every decent shot they ruffled her hair with their applause, or patted her on the back. Martina could not fail to notice that the crowd wanted her to prevail. She obviously needed a cuddle.

Oremans, her face burning, out of breath, was scarlet with exertion. Even exhausted she was faster than Martina, who was fitter, but too much older. It was devastating to watch Martina losing this first-round match that was both poignant and utterly gripping. Martina had the grace to run to the net to congratulate her, and then in the heat of the moment, all the frustration came out, and Martina smashed her racket against a chair.

I wished I had a racket to smash too.

It seemed that it was no longer premature to say that Martina had lost it – not just the match, but her heroic edge. The fact was she had played badly. Her reactions were visibly slower. Gone was the fleet, pouncing cheetah.

It was a tournament that would ruin plenty of ageing players. The elegant Mats Wilander, an old man of twenty-nine, went down in the first round to Agassi, the enigmatic clown who was six years younger.

At the press conference, Martina, puffy-eyed from crying, arrived with her foot-long fox terrier KD – the initials stand for Killer Dog which KD so obviously isn't. With the little dog

165

nestling in her lap, Martina answered the first question. It was about the breaking of the racket: 'Well, they don't last long anyway,' she said. 'I should have broken the other one.' That wasn't what she told television. In front of the camera, she was contrite. Perhaps she felt she could be more honest with us. As for the outcry in England over her ill manners, Martina would say during our odd little interview, a few days later, 'I really don't care what press I got. This is my last match I played at the French Open and to go out the way I did, smashing a racket was a pretty minor thing. People smash rackets every day even in practice.'

As she stood there glaring down at me with the hauteur of an empress, it was hard to believe that the mighty one was in the process of falling. Yet despite all those famous victories, it was becoming difficult to ignore the recent string of defeats. That embarrassment in Houston. This smashed racket in Paris. One had a sense of foreboding.

Did it sugar the pill of defeat, someone asked at the press conference, that her Dutch opponent played something akin to serve-and-volley tennis? 'I'm supposed to feel better because I was beaten by somebody that plays more like me? I don't think so. No, I don't feel any better because of that, but I am glad that she plays a more aggressive style than most of the other women.'

'What happened with your game today?'

'I think not having played here for so long, I really wanted to do well and didn't allow myself to play as well as, obviously, I am capable of.' But was better play something she was still capable of? Time was the one opponent you couldn't beat.

Would today's result change the end of her career? 'You mean like I quit today?' She smiled as though it were a joke. Then she told the truth. 'For one brief moment I thought that I should just quit right now, and not have to worry about getting ready for another match, but that lasted for about one quarter of a second.'

Her French Open singles triumphs of a decade and a dozen

years ago would be two of the great memories, did anything supersede those?

'Here?'

'Yes.'

'I think being able to take KD to every restaurant I go to. That is great. I mean, she goes everywhere.' Because of the strict animal quarantine regulations, when Martina played in England, KD stayed with sitters. 'Today I wanted to leave her at home, but she insisted on coming because she is used to going everywhere with me here. Like, "This is Paris, I go with you." So here she is. And now I will definitely have an opportunity to experience Paris. I finally will go to the Louvre.'

— 13 —

A Conversation with Billie Jean

I have been rearranging the furniture on the mezzanine level of the Roland Garros players' lounge for half an hour, trying to make sure that when Billie Jean King finally arrives, the light will not be in her eyes, or in mine. It is late morning in Paris, a couple of days after Martina's defeat. The players' lounge furniture here runs to hard, upright, little wooden chairs and spartan square tables. Every comfort, it would seem, has been spared. And the lighting seems to have been designed by a latter-day inquisitor. I shift a chair a couple of inches, then the other chair, then the table.

Next door to me a tennis player I don't recognize sits beside a copy of Vikram Seth's novel, *A Suitable Boy*, waiting for something. I long to know who she is as she appears to be one of the very few non-slush readers on the circuit. But it seems impolite to say you must be a famous tennis player what's your name. And anyway, she is not actually reading the book; maybe she is just watching it for someone. Before I decide to ask her, she looks at her watch and says aloud to no one, certainly not to me, 'I have to change for practice.'

I get back to the furniture. Downstairs a few players of the second rank are chatting in a huddle and a couple of coaches sit at the bar. Noon comes and goes. I've just figured out how to make the place feel a little less like a police interrogation room when, finally, straight from her interview with NBC, Billie Jean King strides into the lounge, sits down, puts her elbows on the hard pine table and peers expectantly at me. Billie is the shrewdest woman on the circuit.

Now she is high on natural adrenaline, the interviewee's drug. A better businessman than most men – Donald Trump made more money but also lost more – she started open tennis for women, and developed and runs multi-million dollar World Team Tennis. The female millionaires on the circuit owe it all to Billie, the quintessential good operator. She's come a long way, baby, and knows it. *Life* magazine named her one of the one hundred most influential Americans of the century. No US president made the list. There's much more on her curriculum vitae. She is a workaholic.

A somewhat chubby woman of fifty, she is wearing an unflattering, puffy white tracksuit, but hell she still looks good. The energy makes her alight. In 1963 as Billie Jean Moffitt, she was the Wimbledon runner-up. She was nineteen years old. There is still the sweetness of mien that caused them to call her Little Miss Moffitt after Little Miss Muffet the girl in the nursery rhyme. Three years later she won her first Wimbledon singles title.

Billie Jean King probably knows more about Martina than anyone else does. Maybe even more than Martina. In some ways it seems likely that Martina has patterned herself on Billie; in others Billie still has something to learn from Martina. They have an awful lot in common. On court, Billie used to shout at herself and at the linesmen; a feisty serve and volleyer, she was athletic and she was the tour's most vehemently outspoken player. This advocate of women's equal rights, however, never saw eye to eye with the feminist politicos, many of whom deplored her money-oriented view of equality. At the Wimbledon 1973 press conference, a female reporter asked the then champion what she thought of being listed as Mrs L. W. King. 'I think that feminists get hung up on too many trivial things,' she replied.

169

The relationship between Martina and Billie Jean King has gone through a series of ups and downs. Its latest manifestation had begun in 1989 with that telephoned call for help, the one that led to the Wimbledon 1990, the victory Martina stole from fate.

'I saw you practising with Martina before the singles match, and I happened to be sitting across from you during the match. You were chewing your fingernails.'

'I always do.' Billie Jean King knows I am here to talk to her about Martina. Billie does a lot of interviews for Martina.

'She's been amazed that you have helped her to attempt to surpass your Wimbledon overall record.' Martina has said so to platoons of press.

Billie smiles. 'Well, I think I'm gonna tie her legs together on that one. Tell her, can you give me a break, leave that one for me. No, no, if she wants to break it, that's OK.'

Taking a puff of air, she hunches forward over the spartan wooden table, and launches into an anecdote, no breaths between sentences, a wad of information, proffered easily, as though on automatic pilot. Billie Jean King is far more experienced at interviews than I am, and within thirty or forty seconds I feel I am talking with a friend. She needs little prompting. Wimbledon 1994 is just around the corner. Next month. Despite the pasting Martina has just had here in the first round from the chubby Dutch girl Miriam Oremans, Billie Jean King has to get Martina through it.

Billie remembers their first meeting, the year of Martina's first Wimbledon, but she isn't quite certain just what year that was. 'She'll tell you, she knows exactly when. Her memory's better than mine.'

'Oh, because you were the one who was famous?'

'No, I paid attention to it. She just has a better memory than I do in general. I remember kind of like events, but she remembers dates and addresses. We're different in how we remember. I can remember events and my feelings. The first ball I ever hit. My first tennis lesson, which was the second time I ever hit tennis balls, I knew I wanted to be the best in the world. I knew exactly. I can remember the day. There was clear blue skies, no clouds, eucalyptus trees, two cement courts at Houghton Park. I got in the car with my mom. I was jumping up and down on the seat. I remember we had a green DeSoto. Four-wheel drive, click, click. I was eleven. I said this is what I want to do with my life. *I've found what I want to do*,' she says, elongating the syllables of these seven words for emphasis. 'Mom, I love tennis. I want to be the number one tennis player in the world. She goes, "Oh, that's fine"' – Billie Jean raises her pitch to mimic her mother's voice – ' "but you have homework and your piano lessons." I say, Mom. I know this is it. *This is it.*'

'And you did it. People decide but—'

'Martina felt the same way.'

'Not everybody carries it through, do they?'

'Well some of us don't have the ability. I mean, I have good genes. My parents were really good athletes.'

Martina is always talking about her good genes too. All she and Billie Jean mean is that sport runs in the family – they have inherited good coordination and what is called 'good hands'. 'I wanted to change sport too,' Billie Jean King is saying. 'What I did off the court was almost more important than my performance.'

'I think it was in a way more important.'

'It was to me,' the holder of six Wimbledon and three US Open singles titles says. 'The original nine who were willing to get suspended, we were willing to lose it all to start something.' They started what has become the WTA women's tennis tour. 'Anne Jones came on – if she had been in the States she would have been one of the original nine. As soon as we started it and knew we were gonna have a tour, Anne Jones and Frankie Durr were there. We were out there and we loved tennis,' she says.

'Some years ago, I did a piece for a magazine and I asked Martina whether tennis had changed the image of women in sport and she said—'

171

'Tennis is basically the leader,' says Billie. 'We were the leaders. For acceptance.'

'And I think Martina has been extremely brave for example in the lesbian—'

'Yes, very brave. But she tends not to examine very much before she says something. And then she gets a backlash.'

'What do you mean?'

'Most people would examine in more depth what is the consequence of something. She tends to just say it, and then there's a lot of consequences sometimes.'

Someone interrupts us to tell Billie a lunch meeting is starting.

'OK, I'll be up there in three minutes.'

'Your life is very public. Do you think the difference in the way that you and Martina approached the gay issue is the gay rights movement?'

'The difference in my life and hers is I always had a business going on, so every time I said something it affected many people around me directly. Financially. Besides affecting me financially. For her, she is her own business by herself. Also being younger, she can still go on playing tennis. I have told her for five years, get your money, your financial things in order because after you play, because of your sexual preference you're not gonna have the opportunities Chris Evert's had.'

'It really is still that way in the States?'

'Oh it's terrible. Well you can ask her. It's very "in" right now to be gay or lesbian or bisexual, I guess, but it's only "in" to a point. You don't get endorsements because of it. You get appreciation from, I think, people who have had to go through a time of questioning about their sexuality. But she never had to go through that, yet they have made her a hero. Their hero.' Her tone is thoughtful, almost envious. 'It's quite interesting. And yet she didn't have to go through – there was never a doubt in her mind, she said, as a youngster. So for her it has been very—'

'There was never a doubt of what?'

'Her sexuality. She always knew. Since she was four. She

knew from kindergarten. She had a crush on the teacher,' Billie Jean says.

'People have crushes on a teacher and they get married and have eighteen kids.'

'No, she said she knew. It's a shame to have to go through that stuff and all the struggle,' Billie adds.

'The coming-out struggle?'

'Yeah. She just goes, "What's the deal?" I'm going, don't you realize that people go through a lot of struggling – like whether they're gay, or lesbian, or whether they're bisexual, or what? She says, "No." I said, well lucky you.'

'With you it was more complicated?'

'Oh much more complicated.'

'And officially you've not said anything; am I right?'

'I think with the lawsuit that was pretty official. The palimony thing.'

'Since then are you officially bisexual?'

'Yeah.' So far as I know, though, not since her autobiography has the subject been talked about by her seriously in print. There she spoke of one affair with a woman and called it a mistake.

'You're not officially lesbian, right?'

'I'm probably bisexual.'

'Right. Personally, I think everybody is and the world is structured so that we wind up living our lives largely in one or the other.'

'One or the other. I agree with that,' Billie says. 'Some people have softer boundaries than others, I think. But it's been unbelievable suffering and examination for me, and I think I'll probably continue to examine it.' She chuckles. 'Martina says, what's the problem? I say, OK that's you, everyone's different. You know, I have businesses, my consequences are different.' Billie Jean is thoughtful. 'Like she's on her own. That's what's keeping me. I've always been in business. I always have to deal with, like if I do x, y or z, I've got payroll to pay, I've all these other people involved, I've got causes I want to make sure happen as far as tennis, and there is a very fine line.'

'I agree. You want to live in the big world too.'

'Yeah, I do. But still you have to be true to yourself. To be true to yourself is the most important thing. I'm totally dedicated, the truth is like major to me.'

'Give me one more minute, I know you've got to go. When you decided to play doubles with Martina, how did you invite her to be your doubles partner?'

'We played Wimbledon in 1979, I don't know how we decided to do that.'

'You took her under your wing in the early days.'

'I helped her a little bit, not really, to a point. But I helped Chris a lot too, I helped both of them a lot, and I think I said, do you want to play doubles? Of course she did. You know we were pretty good. It's too bad I'm old. If I had been younger, if we had been closer in age, we probably could have been the best team ever without any question.'

'Now I'm going to ask you a difficult question. You read Rita Mae Brown's novel *Sudden Death*.'

'I didn't read it.'

Someone else interrupts.

'What?' says Billie. It is suggested she get to the lunch. As she doesn't budge, they tell her the suite number. 'OK,' she says, 'I know where it is.'

I continue, 'Rita Mae has written in a rather nasty character in the book, whom she calls Mrs Reilly, who's a womanizer. The character has previously dumped the young Argentinian player who is a lesbian serve-and-volley player like Martina, and a lot of people have said Mrs Reilly is meant to be you.'

Billie's eyebrows reach to the sky.

'Do you want to say no, it's not you? All I want is a denial.'

'Me? No way.'

'Right. You were not a great womanizer who took people and spat them out?'

'No. I don't know who they're talking about, it's not me. I'm just the opposite of that.'

'She also implies that you were Martina's first.'

174

'That's Rita Mae. Rita Mae and I never got along.'

Her dislike of Rita Mae is, shall we say, unreserved. As I have mentioned, Billie blames the break up of her and Martina's doubles partnership not on Martina but on the influence of Rita Mae who has denied it was down to her. Nor did the shooting incident which marked the end of Rita Mae's relationship with Martina do anything to endear Rita Mae to Billie. 'She almost killed Martina,' Billie says. 'Missed her by inches.'

'Rita Mae says it was an accident,' I explain. 'She threw the gun and it went off when it hit the ground.'

Billie is unimpressed by my protestations. The shot could have killed Martina and for Billie that is the bottom line.

As we are in dangerous territory anyway, I now ask, 'Did you have an affair with Martina?'

'No.'

14

Endgame

'Martina is a very black and white person,' Ana Leaird said from behind the high counter of the WTA office at Stade Roland Garros in Paris. For fifteen years now Leaird has been doing publicity for the WTA. Nuances, says Ana, are not Martina's big thing. 'She once wouldn't talk to *USA Today* for two years because she didn't like something they wrote about her. If Martina decides she doesn't like you, she doesn't like you. When she cuts, she cuts.'

A couple of days after my interview with Martina in Paris, I bumped into her walking alone on the esplanade at Roland Garros without her security guards. She had no need of them. No one was around. Everyone was watching the match. It may even have been the Sampras–Courier match. When she saw me, Martina didn't cut, she nodded hello politely. I nodded back. In fact all through the season, she never cut. She would never be a pal, but at the press conferences, she answered my questions thoroughly. She did her job, she was a professional. I would never have the opportunity, though, to tell her that I hadn't realized until we were face to face that the interview was being forced on her. She probably wouldn't have cared anyway. There were too many journalists, and too many agendas being foisted on her. She preferred to think of the media, with a few long-known exceptions, as 'you guys', an Americanism which included us women. 'Actually, I enjoy these press conferences under better circumstances, most of the time,' she had said at the one immediately after her first-round defeat. As I would see for myself and hear from my colleagues, it was the WTA that was into barbed wire and fences.

'Massage, that is the secret of a relaxed interview,' Judith Elian of *L'Equipe* tells me too late. As for another face to face at a more propitious moment with Martina, the answer from the WTA is no.

At Edgbaston in England for her pre-Wimbledon tune-up, the other Old Lady of the circuit, 31-year-old Pam Shriver, was told by the world number 71, 22-year-old Rachel McQuillan, who refused to shake hands at the end of the match, that she was 'old, haggard and should retire'. Shriver had won the match. Pam still isn't quite sure when she is going to hang up her racket. 'I don't have to face that yet,' she had told me in Paris. In England, she repeated that she had no firm plans of quitting, 'though I say to myself every day, "I'm old and haggard and should retire."'

When Martina retired, Pam would have the most doubles wins of any active player on the tour. In that sense, she would again be number one. 'I wouldn't play it because of how many titles I have, I think I would play it because I felt I could still contend in the grand slams. But the idea of just playing doubles and travelling full time on the tour – it's not an easy life to do that and just play doubles.'

'That's what Martina has decided, isn't it?'

'When I talked to her in Amelia Island, I think she had thought that maybe that was gonna be difficult to do.'

'For the reasons you're saying?' I asked.

'I think also the sport. If you only play doubles – the sport is very funny, it kind of looks at doubles only as though you're not a complete player, and let's face it, Martina should be seen as anything but that. So I don't know – you have to deal with things in your own ego, and you have to feel whether or not playing doubles is worth doing, and whether or not it's better to just move on.'

On 4 June 1994, a Friday, that notorious episode of the 'Roseanne' television series, in which she goes to a lesbian bar and gets kissed, was finally shown on British TV. A number of American stations that usually broadcast the programme had dropped that one. Roseanne goes to the bar with her nervous sister, who is pregnant. Both are straight. There are all sorts of women in the bar, some of them masculine-looking, some not. Roseanne, who is kissed by a gorgeously feminine Mariel Hemingway in a mini skirt, doesn't enjoy the kiss, but she does enjoy the bar where she flirts outrageously with the female bartender.

'What are you doing?' says her appalled sister, who hopes pregnancy will protect her from being mistaken for a lesbian.

'I'm doing what I always do in a bar,' says Roseanne. 'Trying to score free drinks.'

The next night, Martina and some friends went to London's most fashionable lesbian bar, Wow, in Covent Garden. It was close to midnight when they arrived. The woman on the door waived the entrance charge. The place wasn't packed, but it was a bar on a Saturday night. Hardly the place to go if you wanted quiet and calm, no cigarette smoke, and to focus on tennis. Eastbourne was starting in a week, Wimbledon in two. On some level, surely, Martina had written off her chances. She knew better than anyone when she was playing well; she also knew when she was playing bad or mediocre tennis. Martina Navratilova was after all the consummate professional.

At the bar, Martina was immediately recognized but very few of the women there dared to intrude. One young woman said hello, and then, abashed at herself, asked, 'Do you ever get pissed off when people you don't know come up to you?'

'Yes,' Martina replied. She was used to direct questions which were supposed to be answered directly. It was no more than that. But the young British woman felt slapped. English manners are different.

As the story made the rounds, people got madder and madder. 'If she doesn't want to be recognized,' said one erstwhile admirer, 'why does she come to a place like this?' Very carefully, however, no one mentioned anything to anyone who might mention it to the tabloids. Martina's sexual preference was no longer news, but a visit to a lesbian bar on the eve of Eastbourne and Wimbledon was a story the tabloids would have run with.

The rites of succession are brutal in tennis. One murders one's predecessor on court. In 1975, Martina summarily executed the brawniest powerhouse in women's tennis, Margaret Smith Court, on her own turf, winning the quarter-final of the Australian Open in straight sets. In 1978, Chrissie had her dismal day, bludgeoned 2–6, 6–4, 7–5, in the Wimbledon final.

In the next decade, Martina Navratilova became the greatest female tennis player the world has ever seen. Whatever difficulty she had had in finding her killer instinct, now she was as ruthless as Chrissie and Billie, as she had to be, kicking aside all other idols: Billie Jean King eluded her until the drizzly 1980 Wimbledon quarter-final, when she too fell to the ground, full of excuses. 'I was up 5–1 in the tie-breaker, but my glasses were all wet, and Martina came back and won the set.' The match was halted. The next day, in mid-match, the glasses broke and she had to switch to the duplicate pair. 'No two pairs of glasses ever feel the same, and Martina finally beat me,' she wrote in her autobiography. 'I think that may have been the single match in my career that I could have won if I hadn't had bad eyes.' Good losers are rarely winners.

Martina dispatched a great many more, equally unwilling. Old champions don't just fade away.

In 1994, at Eastbourne, a tournament which Martina had won eleven times – twice more than Wimbledon – a 23-year-old nobody had heard of became the woman who shot Jesse James. 'I realized I was playing a legend,' said Meredith McGrath after she ambushed Martina in the quarter-final.

The crowd last saw Martina running what she suddenly saw

as a gauntlet, from Centre Court to the locker room, briskly, tearfully, and looking no one in the eye. Later, at the press conference, her racket hand was heavily bandaged. 'I feel pain,' she said, 'but it has nothing to do with this hand.'

Gert had cried after Martina's Paris defeat, and was now crying in Eastbourne. This time, the plastic admission pass secured for her by Martina proclaimed simply, guest. Even to loyal Gert, the thought was surely becoming inescapable that like the woman in the song Martina had stayed too long at the fair.

On the day of the final, Gert was still in Eastbourne because Martina was still there too. Martina had planned to be in Eastbourne all week, playing and practising. Now she was just practising. Fooling around, partnered by her coach Craig Kardon in an ad hoc mixed doubles exhibition against Patty Fendick and a man of a certain age in bermuda shorts who the gathering crowd thought must be Fendick's coach. They didn't really care. They were there to see Martina.

In the final that afternoon, Meredith McGrath was playing a tennis twin, Linda Harvey Wild, also an American from the Midwest who also had a world ranking in the mid-thirties. Both were twenty-three. Harvey Wild's greatest claim to fame was that she too had once beaten Martina here in Eastbourne, in 1992.

Gert did not deign to watch the match. She sat outside in the sun. Gert, curled up on the grass outside the entrance to the Centre Court during the match, listened sadly to the cheers that once had belonged to Martina. McGrath won. 'At least Martina lost to the person who won the tournament,' Gert said.

The final was hard fought and more than moderately interesting, but the real news of the tournament was that Martina's last final had failed to happen. The elation that usually follows the final at Devonshire Park was muted. The mighty Martina had lost her crown and she would never regain it.

'It's truly the end of an era, isn't it?' said a middle-aged male spectator in a battered Panama hat. Then, hope suffusing his voice, he added, 'But this new girl is something, isn't she?'

The queen is dead, long live the queen?

'I admired her,' said a woman who had seen Martina win here eight times, 'but things end, don't they?' It was because of age that, lumbering like a mama bear approaching winter, *slow*, Martina had been clubbed in the first round of the French Open and bushwacked here.

Billie Jean King told Martina, 'This year is a bonus. Remember, you almost quit, before.' 'This year is a bonus,' Martina would say. Everything that happened this year was more than she had expected, so it was all good, even the bad. That's what she would tell the BBC and the rest of us. That's what she would try to tell herself.

Virginia Wade popped into the press tent from time to time. As in her days on court, she always seemed to be moving fast. The former Wimbledon champion is now one of BBC television's tennis commentators. In my view, the best one.

Another BBC employee, the director who was in the midst of making the authorized television documentary 'Martina – Farewell to a Champion', was not very happy. Martina's defeat in the quarter-final had ruined the plans for filming her playing the next day. The camera positions were better at Eastbourne than at Wimbledon. You could get closer. Anne McArthur and I were giving the director a lift home and we were waiting for her to find her crew and give them some last-minute instructions so that we could leave. It was late, about 9 p.m. As we stood on the steps of the press centre, Bud Collins, the bearded Mr Tennis of the American network NBC, came out. He and his wife were finally departing too but stopped to chat. Ten minutes earlier I had bought two of Bud's books, which were hard to find in England but were on sale here in the tennis book pavilion. The erudite bookseller was also the Wimbledon Centre Court steward. Everyone knew that Bud who had been a tennis correspondent for decades was a reliable commentator. Now

Bud told me he was also a betting man. But I will get to that.

On the drive home, our passenger, who was zonked, told us of her amusing encounter with tournament director George Hendon. This was the same George Hendon who had witnessed Pam Shriver's napkin contract with Martina. Our passenger had negotiated for nearly a year to do Martina's Wimbledon farewell, a joint BBC and Transworld (TWI) production. TWI is one of sports agent Mark McCormack's companies. Another is the mammoth IMG which manages many of the players, including Martina. TWI is known for its highly professional, occasionally bland, and certainly unpolitical and uncontroversial sports coverage. It is competent but very middle-of-the-road. The BBC director, on leave from the highbrow 'The Late Show', had radical tendencies which she kept under wraps in all her conversations with the tennis establishment. Even so, it took her eight months to arrange a meeting with Martina, which she says was all of five minutes in the IMG offices. Martina had seemed tense until the director mentioned she too was lesbian. Now she had eight days of shooting lined up, excellent access; but because of TWI's control, her parameters were limited. She was stamped, sealed and delivered, but no fool. 'It's going to be a soft film,' she said, 'I realize that, but at least I will mention that Martina is gay.'

Our passenger had needed George Hendon's cooperation to arrange the filming at Eastbourne. He was very well disposed to the BBC, but he said that they didn't want anything like 'that terrible Channel Four film of a few years ago, nothing on *that* subject.' This was an oblique reference to what was in fact a BBC film called 'Suddenly Last Summer' about the preponderance of lesbian Martina fans at Eastbourne. It was well cut and very amusing, but not if you were trying to promote a conservative, sponsor-driven image. It also, I thought, gave an erroneous impression because Martina's fans are straight as well as gay. The point of the story is that our passenger was the director.

*   *   *

The press prefers wit to compassion. Martina's first ever Wimbledon victory, in 1973, had been against the Briton Christine Truman Janes. *The Times* now suggested that Martina's last Wimbledon victory, if it occurred, might also be against a Briton and in the first round. The draw was such that unless she shot herself in the foot, or ripped a toenail off getting out of the bathtub (as one male player did), Martina should at least get to the fourth round where she would probably face Helena Sukova, whom she might or might not beat.

But on the eve of Martina's final Wimbledon she was playing like somebody's ancient aunt. The weight of the occasion, even more than her waning power, could well prevent success. She wasn't *that* old was she? It was just her nerves were worn. 'It gets worse. And it's not just me – it's any athlete or performer. The older they get, the more nervous they get, the more butterflies they get. So it's not something you can get used to and say, oh, a piece of cake.' At Wimbledon where she was the fourth seed, the draw had been immensely kind, even providing first-round British cannon fodder.

When Martina arrived at this her last Wimbledon, she had already been written off by many in the media. The reports of her death, however, were premature. 'I wouldn't have come if I didn't think I had a chance to win,' she said. She wasn't predicting victory exactly, but she was in the hunt. The quarterfinals? She scrunched up her face, 'Ummn.' No. The semis? Better. And the final? Her dream was still a tenth title, she said.

There were those who laughed.

Yet Martina, the fourth seed at the championships, was also the world number four. At Wimbledon, magic was still, just, possible. Her greatest moments had often been wildly improbable.

～ 15 ～

Wimbledon Homecoming

In the dead of night, Martina pays a visit to her favourite spot: 'Centre Court, when there's nobody here, at night, with just the guard dogs. I was here at full moon,' she says. 'I can feel all those champions out there.'

She is staying at the nearby house where she has stayed the last few years, on Newstead Way. Wimbledon seems like home. As soon as she arrived, in fact, she was a changed woman. That lurking sense of depression vanished. Martina doesn't really have to say it, it shows, but Billie hears her tell Craig, 'I feel good again. I'm happy being on court and it even feels fun running.' Instead of the strawberries and the champagne that Wimbledon sells the punters, or the oversweet Robinson's barley water that is gratis to the press, Wimbledon has provided Martina with a spiritual hypodermic of adrenaline, a 'contact high'.

The change was startling. 'She started this tournament at about as low an ebb of confidence as she's ever started a Wimbledon,' Pam Shriver observed.

'Being at Wimbledon,' Billie elatedly told whoever would listen, 'once again has made all the difference.' Billie, who was working as an anchor for American HBO television, did a lot of other interviews on the state of Martina's mind and body. Unfortunately, she had less time to give Martina here than either of them liked.

'She leaves early in the morning and gets back at eleven-thirty at night doing TV,' Martina complained late in the championships. 'We actually haven't had that much time together. I've done most of it with Craig and on my own. But we still have our talks and she helps me here and there to stay focused on what I'm doing if I start to get a little scattered. I would say she's just been serving as an anchor, but I've been pretty anchored on my own.'

This sounded miffed, but it was also, possibly, meant to be funny. Did Martina mean to imply Billie was just a TV anchor; or an anchor to Martina? Fast on her verbal feet, Martina was perfectly capable of intending the pun.

It is traditional on Wimbledon's first Tuesday, Ladies Day, for the reigning champion to play the opening match on Centre Court. To the consternation of many, but the whoops of more, Steffi Graf lost in her first-round match. This fate had never befallen a Wimbledon defending champion in the hundred and ten years of women's play.

To those who were tired of Graf winning everything, especially now that Monica Seles was out of it – stabbed on court by a maniacal Graf fan – Steffi Graf's departure was a good thing. Good for tennis. Graf, who had won the title five times, but was still only twenty-five, had been defeated by Lori McNeil, a thirty-year-old African-American who in ten visits to Wimbledon had never got beyond the quarter-finals. McNeil was, on her day, though, an excellent serve-and-volley player, one of the last of the dying breed. If she kept playing as well as she had against Graf she might even reach the Wimbledon final. 'This was the best moment I have ever felt in my life,' McNeil said.

For Graf it was one of the worst. 'It hurts to lose. I mean right now I'm very disappointed. I'm not going to kill myself though.' Instead she departed for a holiday at an unannounced destination. As Boris Becker so famously said in a year he failed to win the title, 'No one died. It's just a tennis match.'

For Martina Navratilova, though, Steffi's defeat was a blood transfusion. More. It was the miracle that would make the miracle of another Wimbledon title possible to contemplate. Gert and the rest of the fans were joyful.

Surprisingly, Martina herself wasn't. 'I had really mixed feelings about Steffi losing. My dream really was to play her in the finals. That's what I really wanted, you know. But at the same time I guess it would be easier, if I get there to play whoever, because she's number one. I slept badly after she lost. I kept empathizing so much with what she must be going through, because I certainly went through it a few times earlier this year, losing early. It was funny, a strange feeling. I've never had that before, or to that degree for somebody else.'

The only two superstars in women's tennis had practised together in the days before Wimbledon opened officially. 'I'm not going to talk about that practice session,' Martina said at the press conference. 'We had a blast.' Steffi couldn't be reached for comment. 'We've never done it before,' Martina continued. 'That's all I'll tell you, and I'm sure we'll do it again before I quit.'

'Does it make you more nervous with her out and everybody expecting you—'

'You think I can get more nervous than I already am? Not possible. I was hoping that Wimbledon itself would just take over and it has. So I'm rising to the occasion, I think, rather than wilting from it.'

Bud Collins of the American television network NBC walked into the press conference late.

'That was a good quote, you got here just in time, Bud — "I'm rising to the occasion rather than wilting from it." I've got a joke about that, I'll tell you later. It's a clean joke. Do you guys want to hear it?'

I didn't. Time was too precious at the press conference. At any moment one of those silvery-haired Wimbledon types could call it quits. Quickly I interjected a question about her serve. 'Have you done anything to work on it recently?'

'I set up targets and hit a lot of serves, probably a hundred serves, but even that little makes a huge difference, the repetitions. When things go wrong, it's the toss that goes off. Because I hit enough serves, the toss, even if it goes off a little bit, the whole serve doesn't. It's just a matter of reminding the body of what it's supposed to do enough times. I don't have to do it that much but I need to do it some.'

'A hundred times a day, or a hundred times between the matches?'

'Just on the days off when I don't play a match. Not necessarily every day. Yesterday it was so windy it was pointless to practise serves. I actually ended up going indoors.'

There would not be the hoped-for climax of Martina facing Steffi in the final. Nor the fear of defeat that such a match would have generated in Martina's fans. It is salutary, though, to remember that the Navratilova–Graf match record remains 9–9. Martina's most recent triumph over Steffi had been in 1993, the previous season, in Tokyo.

Who knows, maybe Martina would have won the dream final.

With her back to the royal box, Martina serves. The motion is still gorgeous though her power has lessened. In this her first match, she begins, gently, to dispatch the young Englishwoman. Two lines of fifteen to twenty photographers face each other like opposing armies from each side of the court; but their weapons are aimed at Martina. They will be at every match. As she looks out over the court Martina can see the eighteen stripes of mown grass, cut so that light alternates with a darker green.

Perhaps partly to show up the French, the British put Martina on Centre Court for her first-round match. Claire Taylor, the nineteen-year-old whose first Wimbledon singles it was, looked very small against Big Mama. The crowd, which had given Martina a standing ovation on her arrival, was soon cheering for game Taylor, who was outclassed but showing a willing heart. Far from being unnerved, Martina smiled benevolently whenever Taylor made a good return and even complimented her aloud on a winner. Then, tenderly, almost fondly, 6–2, 6–3, Martina swept her away.

Martina's arm was iced and wrapped after the match. 'It's fine. It's just precautionary. I've had a bad wrist for three years now, but if I do this it feels better. And then my thumb started hurting a couple of months ago. I started icing it and it got better.'

'After every match you do that?'

'After every match, yes.'

Centre Court is already noticeably chewed up behind the baseline as Martina arrives for her second-round match. It is only the first Thursday of the two-week tournament. The grass was slippery at the beginning of the week and still is at the outer edges, but now a heatwave seems about to descend on London. In hot sun the court will become hard and slow, the normally wild bounces almost as reliably tame as clay. The two ball girls kneel at the right of the net; the linesman sits with his green sports jacket slung over his chair.

The umpire too is in shirt sleeves today. How different from yesterday and the day before when winter was in the air. The Duchess of Kent is not in her usual place in the royal box. She missed Martina's first-round match on Monday, too, which started after six.

Martina's second-round opponent is the 29-year-old Italian Sandra Cecchini, who has a bad back. In less than an hour Martina dispatches Cecchini, whose only damage seems to be to Martina's racket. Fingering the strings dubiously during the match, Martina finds that the racket is broken and switches to another. When the match finishes, Cecchini asks for Martina's broken racket as a souvenir of the match. 'I was looking around for a kid to give it to, and there were no kids down there. Funny thing.'

Sandra says, 'I want it.'

'OK.'

In the third round she faced another young crock, 23-year-old Linda Harvey Wild, the one who beat Martina in Eastbourne in 1992. She is wearing an enormous knee support. She hurt her knee at Wimbledon three years ago. Unlike the previous two, Harvey Wild could play on a good day. Today she is good enough for Martina to show off a few shots that are tellingly angled on the way to the easy 6–3, 6–2 victory.

What is sad is that we are so elated that she has survived. We have been so frightened; she has been playing such terrible tennis. Until now. Is Martina peaking at just the right time?

As she walks off the court, Martina's eyes search the stands for a child. She wants to give away the official pink towel with the lavender stripes she used during the match. She hates these towels, which they have given the women this year, yearns for the traditional green ones. Her advice to the tournament: 'Give the guys pink towels.' But the fans, she knows, are not fussy about the colour of a souvenir. There – she tosses the towel into the Centre Court stands. As she leaves, there are of course autograph hunters. The crowd that trails her everywhere is showing an admirable British restraint. In the stands, though, they applaud like Italians.

Any match with the six-foot two-inch Helena Sukova was complicated for Martina. She could never forget that it was Helena's mother Vera, the Czech national coach, who was blamed for Martina's defection.

'Do you have any special feelings when you play her?'

'Yes, to beat her. She beat the pants off me a few times, beat me at the US Open last year.'

Sukova was a nemesis. Of their twenty-nine matches, Helena has won only five, but they have tended to be at crucial moments of Martina's career. Sukova had done her more harm than anyone apart from Chris Evert. It was Helena who ended Martina's record 74-match winning streak and stopped her from completing the Grand Slam by defeating her at the 1984 Australian

Open. It was she who butted Martina out of the 1993 US Open. It was conceivable she could put an early end to what was at last becoming Martina's farewell party. Were there any negative thoughts, someone asked Martina. 'Have those and you're dead,' she said.

'That's gonna be a real test,' Pam predicted of the match.

In fact, it wasn't. Only in the fourth game of the second set did we see Martina making magic with a jump smash accompanied by a yelp. There was no need for magic before or really after. Three-quarters of Martina's first serves went in, not bad, and almost all of them deftly angled. But she needn't have bothered. Helena Sukova played like a praying mantis: long and calm, static when she should have been running. Martina won, 6–1, 6–2, in just forty-three minutes. 'I've never handled Helena like that before.'

It helped winning easily, because it meant she didn't have to worry about any aches and pains when she woke up. 'It's nice to have an easy one physically like that because playing back to back I don't have the day to recover. It sets it up nicely physically for tomorrow at least.' Tomorrow she would be playing the other Czech, Jana Novotna, in the quarter-final. Novotna was now the bookmaker's favourite to win Wimbledon. 'I'm going to try and get through with the press as soon as I can and take care of my body and just start getting ready for [tomorrow's match] mentally. But I'm sure I'll be thinking about what happened last year.' Last year Martina had lost to Jana in the semi-final.

The bookmakers had cut the odds for a tenth title from 16 to 1 at the start of Wimbledon to 5 to 1.

'Is that ice you have on your wrist?'

'It's ice. I just put a little bit on my wrist after I played. It's just preventive, it's fine. Everybody's been asking me that question at least once.'

Do they care about her, or do they want to make her think they care about her? Or do they need a detail to enliven a story? The answer to all three is yes. Who is going to inquire about her sore wrists devotedly when all this is over? And to whom will she dispense largesse? After the quarter-final a little boy ran on to Centre Court for her autograph. Pleased, she tousled his head and signed her name for him. Again she hurled the used pink towel into the crowd where a man, delighted, caught it and kept it.

It had been crowded in the one-on-one interview room with little Arantxa Sanchez Vicario. The WTA had told the Wimbledon authorities who told me – that was the chain of command – that Arantxa, the world number two, had refused an interview for the profile I was doing for the *Sunday Times* because she was too busy. It became apparent at the press conference that no one had asked her, and she agreed to a private interview on the spot. 'If you are trying to be the best player in the world,' she said in the windowless, basement Wimbledon interview room, 'you really have to be aggressive so I just thought that I had to improve my serve which has not been my best of weapons. In practice I serve maybe two hundred balls every day and I can now make aces.'

Martina, older and perhaps wiser, was unleashing only a hundred practice serves a day.

Now in that same little room where I had been with Arantxa we were three, Sue Mott the *Sunday Times* tennis correspondent, Jana Novotna and me. The room with its hospital-green walls is surely not much more than six by six. Jana Novotna, who is single, had a gold band on her wedding finger and wore an expensive watch. I didn't ask about the ring and tried not to stare at the watch. At that close range I could not help but examine the lank flaxen hair, which she wears pushed back out of the way. The face was pale, washed out, the blue eyes pale too, but the 25-year-old's intelligence was glowing. Jana Novotna is a woman who is not afraid to talk. Perhaps this is a Czech quality. Martina, she said, had had no influence on her at all. She had defected before Jana was even interested in tennis. Apart from Martina, Jana Novotna was the best serve and volleyer in the game. Some said she was now better than Martina. She had career wins over everybody including her doubles partner Arantxa, Monica Seles and Steffi. At the end of the 1993 season, Jana's total prizewinnings reached three and a half million dollars. Although only thirteen women have earned even three million dollars in prize money, Martina, still number one on the Money List, has won twenty million. Beating Martina in the previous year's Wimbledon semi-final had been a milestone of Jana's career.

'It was the first time I play on Centre Court; nobody talks about that,' she said. 'Nobody mentions I was not scared of that.' This is a reference to the next match she played, the final, which is regarded as perhaps the greatest ever 'choke' in women's tennis. Jana, staring at victory over Steffi Graf, didn't like what she saw, and promptly forgot everything she knew about playing tennis. She lost her nerve; choked. Graf won. Novotna ended the championships crying on the shoulder of the Duchess of Kent, a photograph that whizzed round the world.

Jana has always denied she choked; she denies it again now. 'I would have choked in the first set, and I was winning,' she says. She insists she was merely outplayed by Graf, who in Jana's version rallied brilliantly towards the end. Proof she didn't choke, says Jana, is that she beat a bigger champion. 'Martina was still good then,' Jana says, 'but now' – she shakes her head – 'we were practising together in Eastbourne, she's not hitting the ball hard enough, she's missing shots.' Nothing at Wimbledon had changed Jana's impression. 'I think this year is too much for Martina. Her will is there but her body can't do it any more.' The message from Jana – though she didn't quite use the words – was that Martina is over the hill.

'I looked like a fool for a while,' Martina admitted when Jana's views were put to her, 'because I hadn't played that much on grass and played on clay for a long, long time. It helped because I had so many balls on clay.' That had been the strategy, to 'get down in the trenches, like Billie Jean says'.

*   *   *

192

To calm her nerves before the quarter-final against Jana Novotna, Billie told her, 'You have to stay in the now.' Martina was having terrible butterflies before the match. But Novotna was capable of beating her at her own game, and Martina knew it and was in a state. 'Like I'm not here, I'm not here.'

To help her stay in the present and elude her fears, Billie asked her about the wallpaper. 'What do you see on this wall?'

'Striped wallpaper.'

'What colours?'

'That, you know, just got me in the now. That's all you have to do. It's easier said than done. I've been practising it for a few years now so I can get in it immediately. Just stay with the ball, stay in the now. What time is it? Now. Where are we? Here. That's the whole ball game. You can talk all kinds of psychological babble, but that's basically the bottom line – stay in the moment.'

The wallpaper story was at first glance a little off the wall. 'If she'd started to tell that to me on a change-over five or six years ago,' Pam Shriver, her former doubles partner, observed, 'I'm not sure I even would have got up from the chair. I'd go, like what?' But staying focused on the ball and the moment, however you did it, was desirable. 'She makes a great deal of sense,' Pam added, 'it's true.'

A complication, though, was that it was also necessary to be able to visualize the moment after the match when she was victorious, and even the moment a few matches on when she would hold the champion's silver platter aloft. Unless she could really imagine herself as the Wimbledon champion, she might not allow herself to be successful, as Jana hadn't. She would choke. There was nothing shameful in being outplayed; but losing because you didn't allow yourself to win was. No one other than Martina Navratilova has ever won nine Wimbledon singles titles. The record she broke when she won the ninth four years previously had stood for over half a century. Now she might break her own record and achieve ten. Three weeks ago it had been unthinkable. Now we thought, maybe. This one, as Pam and the rest of us now knew, was the match that would be the real test.

In the players' box were Craig and Danda and two overweight women nobody in the media knew. Tracey the fan told me that they were the couple who house sat when Martina was away from Aspen. One of them was wearing the admittance badge that identified her as the singer k.d. lang. k.d. herself, more elegant and slimmer than in the publicity photos, wearing a white shirt over a blue cotton shell and white trousers, was sitting a couple of rows back. k.d.'s first song, which she wrote at fourteen, was called 'Hoping My Dreams Come True'. Many of them had. Like Martina she was a pop culture icon. Martina has been annoyed by the allegation that they were ever lovers. They are good friends.

'This is the first time I've been to Wimbledon,' she told me. k.d. and the rest of the glitterati had packed in for a mere quarter-final because they knew Martina might not survive to go into the semi. This was the match of the championships. Novotna and Martina were the two best serve-and-volley players in the world. Every seat was filled. Pam Shriver, in denim shorts, sat on a scruffy concrete step. There were Michael Stich and his South African doubles partner Wayne Ferreira, and many of the unknowns on the women's tour who had been told this might be their last occasion to see the great one.

'Whoever wins this match will almost certainly get to the final,' said Anne McArthur, 'and will probably win the championship.'

The match was a strange one, not at all what we were expecting. At the second change-over, Martina called for scissors and cut her hair. 'All of a sudden my hair grew overnight and was in the way. You missed it? Well, you'll see a picture of it in the paper tomorrow, I'm sure.' Winning a point, she literally patted herself on the back. 'When you hit a good shot, pat yourself on the back. Craig taught me that one because I'm so hard on myself.' She was behaving on Centre Court as if she were in her own backyard.

The first set could have been anyone's and very nearly was Martina's. 'I had a set point at 5–4 and she aced me. I didn't feel as focused as I wanted to be in the first.' Jana won the set 7–5. This was the first set Martina had lost in the tournament. Oh no. I couldn't stand the tension, and left. 'It's one set,' Martina thought. 'A long way to go.'

In the players' lounge, which is enormous, thirty-six people were watching Martina's match on the big television. Three or four of them were under forty. All the players who wanted to see the match were installed on Centre Court. The people here form the entourages, the parents, the coaches, the friends, and some of the dignitaries who wanted to avail themselves of the air-conditioning as much as the monitor. It was south-of-France hot outside. The only empty chair was beside Margaret Court's sister June, whose first Wimbledon this was. Margaret, married to a Conservative politician, was at home on her farm in Perth, Australia, and is regarded as enemy number one in the Martina camp. There has been bad feeling because of an alleged slur in 1990 in which Margaret Smith Court called Martina a bad role model because she is lesbian. This, said June, was a throwaway line she made off the cuff at the end of a speech. Born-again Christian or no, Margaret wasn't making a big point of it, her sister says. The whole thing was something of an accident. Then the world's press phoned her. 'It got blown up.' This was a new gloss on a rift that has appeared in tennis circles. As we talk, Martina wins a game that takes ten minutes and then quickly takes the second set 6–0.

I return to Centre Court. At Eastbourne she had been playing clunkily. Here no one had stretched her so we had no idea if she could play, really play. In this match with Novotna she was leaping like someone twenty years younger – no, not like someone, like a champion twenty years younger. She was serving well, her returns, whether chipped or driven, were increasingly effective. Novotna had fallen apart. The match had gone on and on for an hour and three-quarters, and then suddenly the last point came. Martina had won, 5–7, 6–0, 6–1. There was a collective gasp as we realized that Martina could really win Wimbledon.

'Where does this match fit into your catalogue of dreams, Martina?' In a magazine ad for a laptop computer, Martina had said she kept a catalogue of her dreams on her computer.

'This is reality. This is not a dream. I'm living it.' But, 'I've had some weird dreams this week, I won't even tell you.' She didn't.

'Billie Jean's title,' I began, 'is tantalizingly close—'

'It's miles away. I don't even know where I am.'

'You've won eighteen titles. Her record is twenty. Will you try to play the doubles next year to break it?'

'I have no idea. I'll certainly play the doubles if I want to play doubles.' And then she added something no one had ever heard before, something few thought she was capable of thinking: 'If there's one record I don't care about breaking, that's one.' During the Wimbledon fortnight, without anyone really noticing, Martina had broken Billie Jean King's record of 265 total Wimbledon matches.

I took the day off from Wimbledon, deciding to watch the semi-final, which was a foregone conclusion, on TV. I needed to stay home and focus; I had a book to write. A couple of colleagues were being my eyes and ears at Wimbledon, and my mouth. They were going to ask some questions at the press conference. Martina took the first two games to love, then the first set, 6–4. It was hardly a wipe-out, but the match was so amiable it occurred to me that maybe she was giving her friend and neighbour Gigi Fernandez a few points to save her embarrassment. That view didn't last long as the world number ninety-nine began chipping and charging rather dangerously. Martina was down 2–4 in the second set when the telephone rang.

The machine answered, but I could hear the caller: 'Hi, Miss

Blue, it's Rita Mae Brown, I got your fax. It's ten-ten daylight saving time, east coast, America.'

I picked it up. 'I'm watching the Wimbledon semi-final,' I said. 'Can I call you back?'

'Who's playing?'

'Martina Navratilova and Gigi Fernandez.'

'How's it going?'

'Martina won the first set, but she could lose the second.'

'Gigi's a good player, she just doesn't believe in herself,' Rita Mae said. We made a date to talk later.

Rita Mae lived in Virginia where she was busy setting up a polo tournament for the coming July 4th weekend. Although Martina's picture had been on the front page of the *New York Times* after her quarter-final victory over Jana Novotna, it was likely that in Virginia horse country the story had received less attention. According to the wire, American TV that morning had been interrupted for live coverage of the American football hero O. J. Simpson's court hearing on the charge of murdering his ex-wife and her friend. At one point you couldn't watch anything but O. J. on American television. It was perfectly possible, I decided, that Rita Mae didn't know Martina was playing in the semi.

When I got back to the match Gigi was serving for the second set. She took the point, then the next. With my stomach suddenly in knots, I understood why Billie was envious of Martina's tears. Now set point. Undaunted, Martina hit a long shot that just licked the line. Gigi, misjudging it, let it go. Martina was back in the match, whittling away at Gigi's lead. Then came a terrifying tie-break, but the set was Martina's, and so was the match, 6–4, 7–6.

There was a cry of elation. Then Martina pressed her forehead to her hand, hiding her face from the camera as emotion welled up. This time she was crying when she won.

'I wanted to get to the final, wanted to have that chance one more time at the title,' she said. 'I'm just thinking about winning. I'm not thinking, this is my last match. I mean it is, but the overriding factor is I have a chance to win one more Wimbledon. What more can I ask for?'

Everyone knew the answer.

The world number three Conchita Martinez had beaten the Graf-killer Lori McNeil for the other place in the final. Conchita who? We know her now, but at the time, not many people did. She was the Spaniard who threw coins in the fountain in Rome. Except to a few aficionados, the pretty, dark-haired, 22-year-old who had beaten Martina in the Italian Open seemed invisible. 'It is a little bit incredible,' said her coach Eric van Harpen, 'that she is six, seven years in the top ten now, and nobody knows her.' It was only her third Wimbledon, but she had been a semi-finalist the year before.

Ladbrokes had tipped Sanchez Vicario as favourite after Steffi went out, but Ladbrokes didn't know its tennis. Anne McArthur did. The author of the *Wimbledon Quiz Book* knows as much about women's tennis as anyone I have ever met. She mentioned Martinez as a danger even before Graf went out. Tracey, the serious Martina fan, who had foreseen the possibility of Martina's fall to Miriam Oremans in Paris, also predicted Martinez a likely candidate for the final, and the word in the locker room after Graf had been dispatched was, 'Look out for Conchita.'

And now Martinez had made the Wimbledon final. Although she had been in the top five for nearly a year and ranked world number three since 21 February, Martinez was overlooked even by many in the media. The reasons were interesting.

The first had to do with tennis. Conchita had never before been in a grand slam final, and except in specialist magazines it was grand slams that got the real coverage. The second reason had to do with ethnocentricity. The media already had a Spaniard, Arantxa Sanchez Vicario, to write about. The American public – or so the wisdom went – was not eager to know about foreigners, especially foreigners who were winning. Even Steffi was not of great interest. The British public, however, had been habituated to reading about tennis champions who were not British, but one Spanish name was enough to digest.

The third reason was, as one of the American women journalists who regularly covered the circuit put it delicately, 'She's not very nice.'

'What do you mean not very nice?'

'Mewshaw wrote about it in his book.' In his *Ladies of the Court*, which has the same title as Virginia Wade's book, Michael Mewshaw, describing events of three years earlier, told of Conchita exchanging a neck and shoulder massage with another young woman while they were watching a match. 'The massage was down to fine strokes. Conchita let her head droop on the supple stem of her neck as the other girl kneaded her scalp and the base of her skull. Then she leaned back between her friend's spread legs,' he wrote. 'Barely nineteen, her teeth still fitted with braces, Martinez had had a career plagued by rumours of lesbianism. Her own coach had accused her of leaving him to go off with a gay girl.' This charge had resulted in lurid headlines in the Spanish magazine *Interviu*. And the day after the Wimbledon final, a British tabloid would run a picture of Conchita out shopping with a friend, and insinuate, wrongly, that they were lovers.

The WTA had become nervous when I talked to Billie Jean King about lesbianism. 'We heard what you talked about,' Ana Leaird said, darkly, never mentioning the L word.

'Billie Jean opened the subject,' I said defensively. 'Anyway, Martina's not in the closet.' My gut feeling was that Ana wished she were.

Not that Ana herself personally had adverse views of lesbianism. She just didn't think it was good PR for the tour which was in need of a new sponsor. Her job was to keep the lid on things. Mine was to lift it off. But if the WTA let in a little light there wouldn't be anything frightening trapped in the lidded jar. Only secrets are blackmailable. Martina and Judy's relationship had been accepted. 'We didn't talk about hiding it or displaying it,' says Judy. 'We simply were.'

The WTA knew that there were other tennis players who were bisexual or lesbian in sexual preference, and they didn't want any probing. Instead of stories about Conchita Martinez, the WTA had been pushing that treacly anecdote about Lindsay Davenport's prom. Conchita, as it happened, knocked Davenport out in the Wimbledon quarter-final. Because tennis was a world of high-school dropouts, the WTA thought it was news when somebody graduated. Debbie, one of the PR staff, even tried to interest me in a second American who was 'tickled pink' to have a high-school diploma. Even *Family Circle* had stopped printing stories like that in the 1950s. Writing for the sports pages, I was looking for what was extraordinary, not what was ordinary about a player, and so was everybody else. Not stories that showed sweetness and light, but those that revealed will and focus and aggression, stories like the one about the practice wall Conchita Martinez used to play against when she was a poor girl growing up in a sleepy little Spanish town. Conchita named her tennis wall 'Martina'. 'When I was ten, eleven, I used to play against a wall. But in my imagination, I was playing against her.' Beating the hell out of your opponent, real or imaginary, that was the stuff of champions.

In the final, Martinez would face Martina and high seas of emotion. There were very few who thought Conchita's ferocious passing shots and that 102-m.p.h. serve would be enough to turn the cresting tide. After all, it would be Martina's thirty-second grand slam singles final, of which she had won eighteen, exactly the same number as Chris Evert. Martina was a veteran of eighty-five singles appearances on the Centre Court. 'This is Conchita's first grand slam final,' Arantxa Sanchez Vicario told me. 'My point of view is that because Martina has much more experience she will win, but,' Arantxa said reasonably, 'it can go the other way.' The two Spaniards had grown up together in the juniors where Arantxa, who had won her first grand slam at nineteen, usually beat Conchita, or so she said. Now Arantxa had two grand slam victories, Conchita none, so in most eyes, Conchita was merely the other Spaniard.

NBC's Bud Collins was none the less betting on Conchita Martinez. 'We have lost a lot of money on bets this season,' his wife told me. Bud just grinned. 'Conchita is a friend of mine,' he said. 'So is Martina.' He neglected to say that he had also told Conchita he thought she could win. There was good reason, though, for Martina to be regarded as the favourite.

Martina reminded us, 'I lost to her a close match in the Italian that I very easily could have won. You know if I had won three points I would have been up a set and 5–0. Instead I lost 7–6, 6–4.' Martina and Conchita Martinez had never played each other on grass and many thought Conchita was likely to be overawed playing the legend on her legendary turf.

On the other hand, Conchita had had all that wall practice. Recently she had also practised with the real live Martina. Despite the difference in their ages they were friends. 'Conchita is a nice kid,' Martina said.

— 16 —

The Last Hurrah

'I know I dreamed something, but I can't remember. But I woke up very fresh.' The night before a Wimbledon final, Martina always slept well. At eight, eight-thirty in the morning, she awoke feeling ready to go. Donning that natty, many-coloured, designer sweater and the fashionably baggy beige trousers that we would later see in the post-match interviews, she left for Wimbledon. With her in the dark blue official car with the Wimbledon logo on its belly were two hulking blue-blazered bodyguards. Danda, her parents and all the others were coming separately.

Martina put on her dark glasses, protection from the sunlight and from the intensity of strangers' staring eyes. Outside the ivy-covered clubhouse, the waiting crowd was enormous. As she got out of the car, she swivelled three-quarters of the way round to face them and gave a little wave. She didn't take off the dark glasses.

Hardly anyone noticed when Conchita Martinez, arriving on foot, walked through the gate, with her racket bag slung over her shoulder.

In the locker room, Martina seemed unusually calm. She had appeared to be more jittery before the quarter-final, even before the semi. Staying in the now, always so difficult, was no trouble.

'Just stay in the moment,' she told herself. You could focus on the thereness of almost anything. 'See this glass, it's almost empty. I mean this is easy. Now it is easy to stay in the moment. It's more difficult at the beginning of the tournament – you look ahead and you have to keep bringing yourself back, but I'm in the finals now, so I don't have to think about anything else but the final. So I am in the now.'

As part of her visualization for this match, Martina focused on the digits of the number ten. There were two, a one and a zero. 'One plus zero equals one,' she heard Billie say. 'Number one. That's a nice number.'

Conchita Martinez preparing for the match was nervous. 'Oh my God,' she thought, 'what am I going to do? I have to curtsy. What if I don't do it well?' Princess Diana, they had told her, would be there.

Now it was time. They were going down to Centre Court. Martina, with Conchita Martinez at her side, led the procession down the pale blue carpeted stairs. Billie, never quite out of the limelight, was following just a few steps behind. Over the doorway was the famous wooden sign with the motto:

If you can meet with Triumph and Disaster
And treat those two imposters just the same

Martina took a breath and strode through the door. This was the last time she would ever again pass under that sign on her way to play in a singles final on Centre Court. She had been coming here for twenty-two years, her private life had been dissected by the press, the tabloids had labelled her, but she loved Wimbledon, and after all these years, the crowd, she felt, cared for her too. 'You just feel the warmth from them. That's pretty special. It's not just respect or liking the way I play the game. I think over the years they've gotten to know me pretty well.' Even the duchess, who had sent her a note, seemed to Martina to be almost a personal friend.

Martina and Conchita walked on to the court. The applause

was thunderous. Princess Diana and her elder son Prince William were in the front row of the royal box. It was not that long since Martina had played tennis with Diana at the Harbour Club. The Duchess of Kent was sitting beside Diana. Martina and Conchita Martinez curtsied. The men in the royal box were taking off their jackets. Official permission had just been given in deference to the sweltering heat. Among this crowd of the famous, the important and the well connected was the ambassador to the United States. Martina looked up at the royal box. 'That's when it hit me, this is the last time.'

Bud Collins was installed behind the glass window of the TV box. I was behind glass too, up high in the radio box opposite. Martina's full entourage was in attendance, Billie seated today in the players' box between Craig and Danda. Further along the row were her mother and stepfather, Jana Navratilova and Mirek Navratil.

'Right now the way she's playing,' Billie had said enthusiastically, 'it's just as good as 1990.' They all had high hopes.

Everything had changed since Paris. A month is such a long time in sport. Even two weeks can be. At Eastbourne, Billie had realized that Martina's chances to win – indeed her chances to get beyond the quarter-final – were poor unless something happened at Wimbledon once Martina got there. And it had. Two things. Graf had gone out, and Martina had undergone a transformation.

This match, announced the well-cadenced voice of the BBC, would be a great and famous moment in tennis history. No matter which player won, it was a classic occasion like Helen Wills Moody's eighth win in 1938, Virginia Wade's triumph in 1977, the Queen's Silver Jubilee year and Martina's own ninth in 1990. It would rank alongside the 1919 Wimbledon when the balletic Mademoiselle Suzanne Lenglen won for the first time against the burly baseliner and seven-times-champion Mrs Dorothea Lambert Chambers. 'To paraphrase the bard,' intoned the sonorous BBC baritone, 'all great tennis fans in

204

England now abed will think themselves accursed they were not here to witness this great day.'

Conchita won the toss and chose to serve. She won the point. As she won the game, to love, Jana Navratilova tugged nervously at her coral dress. Conchita was not overawed by playing in the final, but it could happen yet. Martina had no reason to be terribly nervous. She held her serve. They were both playing very well, Martina taking the risks at the net and chasing the glorious angles, while Conchita from the safety of the baseline sent forth blasts. The game went with the server until in the fifth Martina broke Conchita, who broke back. You are always most vulnerable just after you've broken someone. Immediately Martina broke again. The crowd was transfixed.

Never before in a Wimbledon final had Martina to concede fifteen years, yet the two whose games were so different appeared well matched. But as Martina played to the supposedly weak Martinez backhand, torrential top-spin shots stormed back. As the first set went to Conchita Martinez, 6–4, Jana Navratilova turned anxiously to her husband, and shook her head. Applauding with the crowd, he looked solemn. Danda and Billie, who certainly weren't clapping, looked frightened. Mr Tennis, Bud Collins, watching through the glass window of the television box, felt relief. He had that money on Conchita Martinez.

High up in the rafters of the newscasters' box, the man from ABC was recording every point in little hand-drawn boxes. With a tabula rasa, the blank page of the second set, Martina rallied to a lead. To counteract the dip Conchita was putting on the ball, to ward off the topspin, Martina was staying back on her serves. She was now cleverly varying her shots, too, 'mixing it up'. In control now, she began to win the points and you could see she felt a real momentum.

Then the match was stopped because Conchita had called for a physio. Her pain was in the backside. 'My butt,' said Conchita, 'my glutus is just a little bit tight.' As the physio worked, Martina, play-acting for the crowd, stagily held up a pink official towel to give Conchita privacy from the cameras.

'She's fine,' Martina thought. She hadn't seen anything in Conchita's play that indicated anything seriously wrong. Cured, Conchita returned to the match. 'I knew she would come back.'

Again Martina supplied the momentum. As she won the set, 6–3, Danda jumped to her feet and Jana threw her arms in the air with the same joyous abandon she had shown when Martina won Wimbledon in 1979. Yes, they thought, Martina will win it. Yes, hoped the thousands of people in the stands. Yes, hoped most of the millions watching via the networks and satellite. Yes!

But it just wasn't to be. Probably Martina knew before anyone else. In the third set, as first one, then another ferocious passing shot sliced through Martina's defences, she suspected, then knew for sure that Conchita was playing the match of her life. No one, Martina thought, had ever passed so well, not even Monica Seles. Doing the only thing a champion can do in such circumstances, Martina played on, played hard, played well. On the last point, she rushed for a backhand it was unlikely anyone could possibly meet, and missed it. Conchita, victorious, threw her racket into the air.

Martina rushed to the net, to congratulate the victor, who had won 6–4, 3–6, 6–3. Hugging Conchita, who hugged her back, Martina said to Conchita that she had played well and deserved to win. It was true.

Conchita said, 'I'm so happy.'

She's thrilled, Martina realized. 'The first one is the best. It's such a pure feeling that first time.'

It was somehow fitting that the young champion had beaten the ageing great one, who was, after all, thirty-seven years and 257 days old. It was sad, too, of course, but it was a sign of the health of the sport.

'It's tough, you know,' Conchita said, 'to take the tenth title away from Martina. I'm really sorry to beat her, but I'm really pleased that I did.'

'I have no regrets,' Martina said. 'I gave it all I had. I lost the bloody match, but what a way to go.'

The one-hour, 59-minute match had been tense and tempestuous, a fabulous finale. Someone threw the greatest diva of them all a bouquet of yellow roses. The crowd stood, both disappointed and elated. It seemed the cheering would never stop.

Martina showed Conchita where to stand for the photographers. They posed. They smiled. And now she was crying. Not because she had lost but because it was over. 'I would have cried even if I had won.'

A chapter of her life was closing. The most important chapter. She would never again have this view of the crowd applauding her from Centre Court. Looking up one last time at the royal box, she saw F. W. de Klerk, the Afrikaner who had handed South Africa over to Nelson Mandela peacefully. 'I didn't see him until then.' She bowed tearfully. It was time now to leave Centre Court for ever. Martina bent down and picked a small tuft of the Wimbledon turf.

— 17 —

When the Cheering Stops

The Duchess of Kent would present the trophies as usual, though not to the usual winner. For a dozen first Saturday afternoons in July, either Martina or Steffi had held high the silver winner's plate. Now it would be Conchita. Conchita had not been overawed by the occasion while they were playing, but as they were about to accept the trophies, Martina noticed that 'her feet were going lower and lower. I was like holding her up. She was thrilled, and I was happy for her.' Martina gave her a little push forward.

'Oh no, do I have to speak?' Conchita asked. At many tournaments the new champion said a few words to the crowd.

'No, you don't have to speak,' Martina said.

The duchess was always a pleasure to see.

'Well, we chatted quite a bit,' Martina said, 'because we had been trying to get together and haven't had the opportunity, and she hadn't been feeling very well, wrote me a note on Thursday. She was trying to talk me into coming back next year. She was trying to convince me to play next year. I said no. I've had enough.

'We've been trying to have tea for ten years. So now I'll have the opportunity to do other things and not worry about playing tennis. I'll have a chance to spend some time with her privately, rather than in front of, you know, the whole world out on Centre Court.'

The ambassador to the United States shook her hand, and he started crying.

'What are you crying for?' Martina asked. 'It was so sweet. You know people feel what I feel and it's nice that I can share that. I can bring people closer to Wimbledon through me. They can feel it, and then that will continue when I'm not around. And that's pretty cool, that I can affect people that way.'

Then she and Conchita paraded the silver platters around Centre Court. She held hers tightly. It was much smaller than the winner's, wasn't it? But damn it, she had foxed them all and made the final. She lost, but she had won.

There was standing room only at the press conference.

'Could you share your thoughts with us, Martina?'

'My thoughts? I've been doing that for twenty years and guess what, I'm not going to do that much longer.' That was one of the advantages of retiring.

'Martina, could you sum up in one word how you feel at the moment?'

'One word? Tired. You asked for one word.'

'Martina, a member of the crowd asked are you going to think again? Are you going to come back?'

'You guys keep asking me that, hoping maybe if you ask me enough I'll change my mind. But I really don't think so. I think I've had enough, and this is a nice way to end. And, you know, I've had a great run, better than anything I could have imagined. I have no regrets.

'I'm obviously very sad, but I would have been sad anyway, even if I'd won. I'm also very, very happy, you know. This is a new beginning for me, and I'm looking forward to my life after tennis. I'll be around, I'm not going to disappear off the face of the earth, but I won't have to get ready for matches any more. It will be nice.'

'Could you describe in more than one word how you feel right now?'

'Very tired.' None of her answers was ever merely a joke though to Martina. She continued, 'You know, I lost the bloody match, but what a way to go. You know, I had a great run. I keep repeating myself, but it has been a great run. I'm glad I was able to share it with lots of special friends that flew in just for the occasion. It would have been better if I'd won, but they were all cheering anyway, you know, and we all cried. I said, I'm not crying because I lost, I'm just crying because it's over.

'I'm happy that I got to the finals, because I think not many people picked me to get that far, especially after the way I played at the French. So I'm happy that I got my game together and my head.'

But she was not ducking anything either. 'You know, it was just that one more step and I didn't quite make it. When you write a script you can make it any way you want. If you want reality, you can't affect that. I'm sad that I didn't win, but I'm very proud about getting this far and having had the opportunity. You know, that's all I asked for and I got it.

'It's like a love affair that grows. I loved Wimbledon from the first time I knew about it, and, you know, it's like in a relationship where you love that person more and more the longer the relationship goes on. It gets deeper,' she said. 'And, you know, it's been reciprocated.' The longest, most important love affair of her life was ending.

'What did you do with that little pinch of grass you took away?'

'I just have it.' As she rose to leave, we began to applaud.

'Since when do we applaud,' said a tall man from American radio. Martina left to go to television. Just before the match the BBC interviewer Sue Barker, who had been interviewing Martina all through the championships, had said that Martina was, 'Well, not a favourite of the crowd, but they have respect for her as a great champion, you can't take that away from her.' Still those unexpressed buts. Now Barker expressed surprise to

Martina at the press applauding. 'I think they've clapped before,' Martina said quietly, 'but never that much.'

As the BBC closed its Wimbledon coverage, its star anchorman Desmond Lynam said with sadness and real affection, 'Farewell, Martina.'

And now it was truly over. She was about to become an ordinary citizen. Waving goodbye to the crowd, Martina left Wimbledon to join Danda and Billie and the others of her entourage.

'We'll go out to a restaurant we're planning with all the friends that are here, and the family, we'll go out and we'll celebrate in style,' she said. Would they do anything special? 'Just eat a lot. I don't drink much. I'll have half a beer and be under the table.'

Conchita arrived for her press conference. There was thunderous applause.

'You know, it's tough. She's a really good player, and I'm really sorry, you know, to beat her, but I'm really happy to be the new champion. It was very hard out there because I knew she was so eager to win the tenth Wimbledon. The crowd was great. I'm not going to say it was even, but I didn't have the feeling that they were against me.' And after the match, 'Martina was really sweet.'

At the beginning of the championships, 'I remember some people saying, "Oh, you really can do it, you can win because you play great." And I was like, Yeah, right.' Sceptical.

Who was telling you that you could win?

'Actually Bud Collins. At the beginning of the tournament he told me I could do it and he bet on me, and I was like, well.'

So you felt that much more pressure then?

'No, not at all. It was like, well, he's really going for me so I'd better do it for him.

'Actually I'm so happy that after my match I could meet Princess Diana. That was really unbelievable. She's so sweet and nice that I could not believe it. She said that it was a great

211

match, that I'm a terrific player and she really loved it. I also met her little boy, who is very sweet, and I don't know, it was really nice of her to do that.'

Have you heard from the King of Spain yet?

'Not yet.'

Later, leaving Wimbledon, I saw an enormous crowd outside the clubhouse. 'What are you waiting for?' I asked. 'We're waiting for Conchita Martinez.'

After the match, Craig said, 'You're still a champion.' He gets pretty soft, Martina thought, he's a good guy.

Billie told her too. And it was true.

The rite of succession had been performed ably, and with passion, but without the usual brutality. Martina Navratilova had eluded execution. She had lost but she had not been humbled. Her legend would survive; in years to come, as players and fans reminded each other of the glory days, it would continue to grow.

'I have no regrets,' Martina said. That wasn't true.

In the same week, Prince Charles talking of his publicly failed marriage with Diana had used the same words, 'I have no regrets.' He did, though, and so, friends said, would Martina. Some of those who knew her well felt sure she would think less often of the nine Wimbledon victories than of the one that almost happened . . . In her dreams, which were no longer for publication, ferocious topspin backhands would roar past her ears and swoop down suddenly.

Both on and off the court, the most famous sportswoman in the world, Martina, was the most interesting to watch. She was also, said Steffi Graf, the most interesting opponent. 'I always liked very much to play against her. The way she plays. She is quite something to watch. She has showed so much – how do you say? – athleticism, and she has done so much for tennis, and my personal feeling is that she is such a great person and character.' Martina would be missed 'very badly – not only by the public but also by the players and the press. She is such a personality that she is going to leave a big gap.'

Women's tennis is trying to take Martina's departure in its stride. All they have left, Martina once said flippantly, is 'Steffi and the seven dwarfs'.

'Would it be correct to characterize Chris as your most memorable rival?' asked one cautious journalist.

'Gee, that's a good guess, I mean, come on, I played her eighty times, you know.'

Is anybody second?

'Well, Steffi would have to come second.'

People are always wondering whether with no tennis to play Martina will have enough to occupy her. They also wonder, when the next Wimbledon comes around, will we?

There is no Martina, but there are some fascinating players. Steffi's new vulnerability, if it persists, will make her and the scene more interesting. The aggressive Arantxa Sanchez Vicario and Conchita Martinez, the 1994 Wimbledon champion, are well ensconced, Martina's favourite of the up-and-coming generation, the 1995 Australian Open champion, Mary Pierce, has a fierce forehand, and more. Interestingly, her open manner seems to be an illusion; verbally, she gives nothing away. The advent of the young American Venus and the new Czech-Swiss Martina promise still more. Oh, and Lindsay Davenport who did make the quarter-finals.

When Martina Navratilova retired, tennis lost its most transfixing, most renowned and most acclaimed player. But it is astonishing how quickly people forget. Virginia Wade was lionized when she won Wimbledon in the Queen's Silver Jubilee, a very special British occasion. Two or three years later when she arrived at Wimbledon hardly anyone noticed she was there. The great test which Martina faces now, to become something more than 'the former champion', will require more nerve than was ever necessary on Centre Court.

'I'll definitely miss playing on Centre Court because that's tennis, that's the essence of what tennis is about for me. But I'll be able to live through other people I'm sure and also have lots of memories stored so I can pull them out a bit, think about – 1984, 1994. I have plenty of them to think on and be happy about.'

She had spent the last quarter of a century mainly playing tennis. How would she go on when the cheering stopped? 'I'm worried about her,' I told Judith Elian of *L'Equipe*. 'You don't have to worry about Martina. She has plenty of money and she has plenty of interests.'

Her main interests at first are likely to be political activism and the ghosted mysteries. There will be travel: 'I haven't seen many things in my own country yet, the United States. I haven't seen a lot of Czechoslovakia either.' Africa beckons her too. And there will be more skiing.

With her friendly antagonists at the press conference, Martina mused on the future thoughtfully during Wimbledon. 'I'm sure it's going to hit me when the last match has been played. You know that's when it's going to get scary, I'm sure, for a while. It will be a whole new ball game for me. But I don't know what will happen. I don't know what I will feel, and I'm sure I'll go for counselling to Billie Jean and Chris Evert and say, how did you deal with it? Chris got pregnant right away, so that's one answer, but I want to relax for a while. If I decide to have a child I still want to relax for a couple of years. So I don't know what's going to happen. But I'm certainly looking forward to it. It's scary and exciting at the same time, as is playing tennis.'

After the final, she said, 'I know I can play great tennis but I'm looking forward to the rest of my life, spending time with my friends, family and animals. I've been here so many times, had so many great moments, and had a longer run than I ever expected to have. Tennis is my life and I owe it everything I have. I will be giving back some I'm sure but right now I'm just living it up. Next year? I'm sure I'll be here. I don't know if I'll be doing TV or coaching somebody or just stopping to visit as I'm going through on my way to Greece or Africa; I'll just have a lot of fun next year trying to figure out what I want to do with the rest of my life as far as being a productive member of society, but as far as having fun, I have it all lined up.'

It was Martina Navratilova's dream – one of her dreams – to be recognized as the greatest female tennis player ever. Full stop. The greatest she was, but that full stop will always elude her. The labels, some heroic, some pejorative, continue to stick. The glorious sports champion, the heroine of many, will always be, in some circles, merely the lesbian tennis player. But now, as she focuses on a new role as political ambassador of gay and other civil rights, is that such a bad thing?

Martina has always wanted to be accepted; now she is, for who she is, even in Revnice. Two decades after her defection, she was made an honorary citizen of the village of her childhood. This is an acknowledgement that the Czechs now recognize her as theirs again, the prodigal daughter returned, on her own terms.

The Duchess, the Princess, and the silvery-haired gents of the Wimbledon establishment, the fans, even the hypocrites on the tabloids like the *Sun* have grown fond of Martina, despite class prejudice, social prejudice, and chronic xenophobia. She didn't give in. Her pooh-poohers did.

When the American branch of the United Nations fiftieth anniversary board was seeking a committee to promote the UN ideals of human rights, social justice and peace, the only sport star's name on the list of distinguished names was Martina's. How many other contemporary sports figures have figured so large in public life?

'I wanted to be liked by everybody but I wasn't willing to do what it took to be liked – which is to say absolutely nothing. As soon as you say something you offend somebody. I think the more open I was about my sexuality, the less I cared whether everybody liked me.'

In the end, it didn't matter much what her erstwhile detractors thought of Martina's sexuality or her political opinions or the choices she has made in life. Many of them finally recognized that she was human, imperfect, and much more than a great player. Although Martina's forthrightness cost her millions in endorsement contracts, it won her the respect of millions of people. Some of it was grudging respect, but respect none the less.

There was also real affection. The American fans were remarkably forgiving when after Wimbledon Martina scratched from what would have been her last US Open. She had found it too hard to peak again for another big tournament so soon after the Wimbledon high. Instead, she spent much of that September on a boat casually circling Lake Powell in Utah. You could see her on deck, playing bridge. Four months after the fabled Wimbledon finale, though, Martina did turn up at Madison Square Garden in New York for the end-of-season Virginia Slims tournament, which she had won six times. But the legs were gone; the focus was just not there. Even late in her career she was subject to anxiety dreams. The handle of her tennis racket swells to the ungrippable thickness of a giant sequoia. It shrinks stiletto-heel thin, too thin to grip. The court is made of ice and her opponent is the skating champion Nancy Kerrigan, on skates. At the US Open, a sudden gust of wind lifts her high above the court and is about to swirl her into oblivion when she catches hold of a flagpole and hangs on. There were reports that just as she had practised being an ordinary person out West in Utah, now at the edge of the Atlantic, Martina was strolling unrecognized on the nearly deserted Hamptons beaches. Nothing really helped: she could not re-ignite as she had for Wimbledon.

'Physically I could still play,' Martina said, 'but my heart is tired.'

And so, on 15 November 1994, the twenty-one-year singles career officially ended when Martina was defeated 6–4, 6–2, by Gabriela Sabatini in the opening round.

It didn't matter. The career had been epic, the hero's American send-off long planned. The song they played at Madison Square Garden as a banner honouring Martina was hoisted to the rafters was 'Simply the Best'. As the *Telegraph* said, 'My Way' would have been just as appropriate. Martina's banner will be raised at every tennis match for years to come. At the Garden, only football and basketball players have been the subject of this sort of hullabaloo. It was the first banner for a tennis player; the only banner for a woman.

The morning after the last match, the CBS-TV anchorman summing up her career called it splendid. 'Splendid may not be a word with enough syllables,' opined the network's weather man, like millions of others a Martina fan. He was right. No one had achieved what Martina had in tennis, or was ever likely to: her 167 singles titles, more than any other woman or man in professional tennis, included nine Wimbledon titles, four at the US, three at the Australian, and two at the French Opens – no fewer than eighteen grand slams, six of them in a row. On and off for a total of 381 weeks (seven years and four months), the most complete player ever was world number one. No other woman has held the fort so long, or surpassed her 74-match winning streak. Add to that 165 doubles titles, thirty-seven of them impressively grand slams and the amazing 109-match doubles winning streak. Hers was a glorious career, one marked by exuberance, excellence and risk-taking from the start. But a career that often put her in hot water and at odds with authorities and the public.

The British crowd had not warmed to Martina when at her first match at her first Wimbledon, in 1973, she defeated the Great British Hope. It would take years before they would learn to love her. The Americans were slow, too, no one taking much notice when the chubby seventeen-year-old from Prague put down her ice cream long enough to win her first little tournament, in Orlando, Florida, in 1974. East European accents were hardly the rage, and instead of welcoming her with open arms when, the following year, she sought and received refugee status, the American public gave Martina her first unpleasant label, the defector.

When the most naturally gifted player on the scene failed for years to win a grand slam singles title, many believed she lacked the will – the character – to achieve tennis greatness. The defector, some said, was a choker. That label she put paid to at Wimbledon in 1978. The photograph of the defeated Chris Evert tousling Martina's hair at the net in congratulation is perhaps the first famous international emblem of sportswomanship. Martina would later show the same graciousness to two decades of opponents.

Nothing has been made easy for her. They made her wait the full six years before giving her American citizenship, in 1981. This was the year, amid rumours of lesbianism, she got her third inconvenient label. She was now the bisexual defector. Only with Judy Nelson beside her would Martina, a few years later, drop claims to bisexuality.

Although she has won $20 million in prize money, more than any other female player, and has dwelled in superstardom for nearly two decades, Martina has continued to show a vulnerability that many have found touching. From the start, hers has always been a world full of impetuous certainty followed by self-doubt and double faults. At thirty she seriously considered retiring. At thirty-eight she finally did it.

It is only now, in maturity, when her best tennis is long past and all serious singles tennis is over, that Martina has at last begun to show a calm certainty. While other gay sports stars continue to hide their gayness, she speaks out on gay issues. When, in her adopted state of Colorado, a constitutional amendment was passed that would block laws protecting homosexuals from discrimination, Martina campaigned to overturn the law and won one of her greatest victories when the Colorado Supreme Court struck down the amendment. The issue, one of civil liberties as much as gay rights, could affect the rights of many minorities.

As the mythographer Joseph Campbell wrote in *A Hero with a Thousand Faces*, the hero goes alone and faces things and conquers so that we know what is possible. That of course is what fascinates us about sport: one woman on court publicly facing the demons of defeat. Martina won for us, even as she won for herself. When after her match at Madison Square Garden she said her heart was tired, she did not mean that she had lost heart.

Wisely, the players have elected Martina president of the women's tour players association. We can expect her to speak out at Wimbledon in years to come, either in that role or as commentator or coach, or spirited tennis citizen. And also, perhaps, as a Londoner: Martina says she hopes to spend one week a month in her own house in the city. Her best known political causes, in which she now has the time to become increasingly active, are ecology, gay rights, animal rights, and the protection of young players. No doubt she will continue to fight for equal money and status for the women's game. Perhaps she will even lead women's tennis back into the forefront, making it once again an advocate of women's sporting rights. So, we will be hearing much more from Martina. It is much too soon to say goodbye.

Index

221

222